體會師曰寫般若體畢竟清淨無有一物可得

是名無法可說是名說法

佛鑑和尚示眾舉僧問趙州如何是不遷義州以

手作流水勢其僧有省又僧問法眼不取於相

如如不動如何不取於相見不動去法眼云日出東

方夜落西其僧亦有省又問於山二和尚言句

見得方名道旋嵐偃岳本來常靜江河競注元

自不流此是如如不之義

羅山和尚僧問石霜起滅不停時如何霜云直須

寒灰枯木去一念萬年去冷清絕點去山不契辦

往巖頭處如前問頭喝云是誰起滅山於言下歠

是十分真用意勇猛丈夫却須言切其
不須令吾聖教不為指南
雖然舊閣田地一旦豁來得也不要講坐禪不
動如此...章偈悉皆論
而今...頭頭物物皆菩提長短方圓只
自知後來絲髮不曾教若閉坐禪成底...目起
更...落西
大珠禪師因僧問一切眾生皆有佛性如何師云作
佛用長窮性你戚用是眾生用是眾生性
性無形相隨用...名...經...一切賢聖皆以無我法
而有差別又當...無法可說是名說法禪師如何

直指下
二

Jikji, light from the East III

Note

Jikji,
light from the East
III

Cheongju Early Printing Museum

Foreword

Jikji is the world's oldest extant book printed with movable metal type. A proud item of Korean cultural heritage, the book was inscribed in 2001 on UNESCO's Memory of the World Register.

In the late 19th century, Victor Collin de Plancy (1793–1881), the first French consul (chargé d'affaires) to Korea, purchased the book and took it to France. It was then that *Jikji* began to receive attention. The first European to discover *Jikji* and recognize its value, he was deeply interested in Korean culture and contributed greatly to the book's survival to the present day in France.

Jikji was first released to the public during the 1900 Paris Exposition. The supplement to *Korean Bibliography* by Maurice Courant (1865–1935) was also published the following year, raising interest in Korea's movable metal type printing technology among Europeans. In 1952, *Jikji* was donated to the National Library of France, according to the will left by Henri Vever (1854–1943) who purchased the book in 1911. Then in 1972, *Jikji* was put on public display during a book exhibition held in celebration of the International Book Year. It was through this turn of events that Europeans began to pay attention to the ancient movable metal type printing technology from Korea.

Our new publication, *Light from the East, Jikji III* mainly covers how the book was introduced to France, and later back to Korea, with a focus on the human stories behind the process. We extend our gratitude to the late Victor Collin de Plancy and Dr. Park Byeng-sen (1928–2011), the two main contributors to the rediscovery of *Jikji*, while hoping that this new publication will give readers a novel opportunity to think about the significant roles they played.

December 2019

Oh Young-tack
Director of the Cheongju Early Printing Museum

Table of Contents

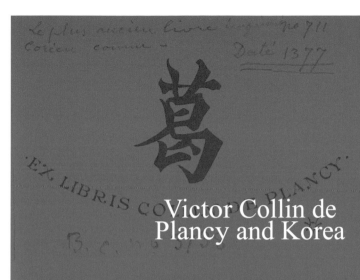

Victor Collin de Plancy and Korea

Lee Hye-Eun

Sookmyung Women's University

Victor Collin de Plancy and Korea

Even before Korea and France established diplomatic relations at the end of the Joseon dynasty, Korean culture had been introduced to the latter through activities by French priests in Korea. After formal relations were established and the French legation was in place, French people began collecting Korean cultural items and introduced more of the Korean culture. In the middle of this process of introducing Korean culture to France was none other than Victor Collin de Plancy (1853-1922).

His family and childhood

Victor Émile Marie Joseph Collin de Plancy (commonly referred to as Victor Collin de Plancy) was a French interpreter, diplomat, bibliophile and art collector. He was born on November 22, 1853 in Plancy (presently Plancy L'Abbaye) in Canton de L'Mery sur Seine, Department de L'Aube. His father, Jacques Auguste Simon Collin de Plancy (1794-1881) was involved in publication and printing. He published fiction and histories after settling down in Paris in 1813. *Infernal Dictionary* (*Dictionnaire Infernal*), which he published in

1818, was so popular that six editions were published by 1863.

The story behind the family name, Collin de Plancy, is a controversial one. The father, Jacques, initially used the family name, Collin Danton, as Jacques's father Edmé Collin married Marie Danton, who was a daughter of Pierre Danton, a mayor during the French Revolution and a sister of Georges Jacques Danton, a revolutionary leader. Jacques used both his father's and mother's family names. After going bankrupt in 1830, he left France for Brussels, Belgium, where he established a publishing company and began publication of a magazine. He moved back to France in 1837, to his hometown of Plancy and from that time began using Collin de Plancy as the family name. He later lost a legal claim against him from a Count Georges de Plancy that he had stolen the name, but continued to use it anyways.

It seems that this issue was not easily settled as "Collin (de Plancy)" is printed in a newspaper from that time.

Jacques opened a new printing and publishing house in Plancy in 1846 named it the Society of Saint-Victor for the Propagation of Good Books and Training of Christian Workers (la Société de Saint-Victor pour la propagation des bons livres et la formation d'ouvriers chrétiens). Until 1858, he mainly published books on the lives and legends of saints to propagate Catholicism.

Jacque's second marriage was to a woman named Gusta Clarisse Bradier, who bore him three children. The first is known to have died

Photo 1: Victor Collin de Plancy (collection of the Médiathèque du Grand Troyes)

a year before the birth of Victor, who was the youngest[1]. A photo of Victor, his second eldest brother, and his father is in the collection of the Médiathèque du Grand Troyes.

The family moved to Paris in 1854, where Victor studied. Studious and diligent, Victor went to L'École de l'Immaculée Conception before studying Chinese at L'École des Langues orientales vivantes.

In March 1877, his law dissertation was reviewed at the Faculté de Paris. With degrees in both sinology and law, he was ready to begin his chosen career: diplomacy.

Career as an interpreter and diplomat

His career with the French Ministry of European and Foreign Affairs began with being dispatched as a trainee interpreter to the

1) Berquet, François, Le Fonds Collin de Plancy à la Médiathèque du Grand Troyes, Roman d'un voyageur: Victor Collin de Plancy, l'histoire des collections coréennes en France, Cité de la céramique Sèvres et Limoges, 2015, p. 72.

French legation in Beijing, China immediately after graduation. His superior at the time, French Ambassador Brenier de Montmoraud, wrote about him in a letter dated March 6, 1880:

> "The student-cum-interpreter in Beijing will someday become an excellent secretary-general. He has a law degree and is very cautious and gentle. I cannot tell for sure but the minister seems to like him and has quickly come to grant him significant favors. That's the kind of impression he's made."[2]

Collin de Plancy wanted to build a career as a diplomat as well as interpreter. But this desire ran counter to the scholarship he received while enrolled at L'École des Langues orientales, which put him on track to be an interpreter. Under these circumstances, his superiors stepped in to help him based on his qualifications and performance, and in the end, he was appointed second consul to Shanghai in 1883.

In May 1887, he visited Korea for the first time, entrusted with exchanging ratification documents for a treaty of friendship between Korea and France. After a short visit, he was appointed the first French consul to Korea and moved there in November of the same year. Except for a brief stay in Beijing as chief secretary in 1890, he

---

2) Brouillet, Stéphanie, UNE CARRIÈRE ATYPIQUE ET CENTRÉ SUR L'EXTRÊME ORIENT, Roman d'un voyageur: Victor Collin de Plancy, l'histoire des collections coréennes en France, Cité de la céramique Sèvres et Limoges, 2015, p. 77.

remained in Korea until 1891 before leaving for Tokyo, Japan where he served as consul. He then served as consul in Washington D.C., Athens, Paris, and Tangier (Morocco) for brief periods, before returning to Seoul in 1895 as minister and consul general until 1906. However, as the Korea-Japan Protectorate Treaty was concluded in November 1905, the Korean government was deprived of its diplomatic rights by Japan, which announced introduction of the Japanese Residency-General of Korea and its Administrative Bureau, and appointed Ito Hirobumi as the first Resident-General. In January 1906, Japan had foreign legations and consulates withdraw including its own. The French legation also left and Collin de Plancy went to Bangkok and retired in 1907.

Collin de Plancy spent 27 years of his 30 years in diplomacy in Asia and 13 years of those in Korea. He was among the last to witness the final days of Joseon (then Korea) and a special witness at that.

Activities in Korea

In 1886, the Korea-France Treaty of Peace, Amity, Commerce and Navigation was concluded. Instruments of ratification were exchanged on May 30, 1887 when Collin de Plancy first visited Korea. However this visit was very brief and he left immediately after an audience with King Gojong. On November 9, 1887, he was appointed the first chargé d'affaires of the French legation,[3] established the French legation in Gwansu-dong, Jongno-gu on June 6, 1888 and stayed in Seoul until June 1891.

Photo 2: The first French legation in Korea

During Collin de Plancy's stay in Seoul, France had neither political nor economic interests of importance in Korea, focused as it was on the Indochinese Peninsula. His main task was to learn of the political intentions of the other powers and collect information. The instructions he received from the French Ministry of European and Foreign Affairs were to avoid becoming involved in conflicts in

---

3) Marc Orange, "Collin de Plancy and French Advisors," *Memory of Seoul: Korea and France 1886-1905* (2006): 92.

Korea; give a favorable impression of French culture to people; give precedence to relations with China over those with Korea; and observe the enforcement of laws that allowed for religious freedom in Korea and react appropriately.[4]

As such, unlike the other powers, France did not actively intervene in Korea's political situation. Against this backdrop, Collin de Plancy is regarded as having led favorable diplomatic relations with Korea's royal court during his time in Korea and played the largest part in bilateral relations. According to *Undiplomatic Memories* (1930) by William Franklin Sands (1874-1946), the American minister to Korea at the time, he was "serious, well-mannered, and discerning." and "never took part in conspiracies."[5]

He was stationed in Japan for about five years between June 1891 and December 1895, before being appointed minister and consul general to Korea in December 1895, beginning his second term in April 1896.

Some record of the background to his return to Korea can be found in Bishop Mutel's[6] diary[7], in an entry dated August 27, 1895:

---

4) Lee Eun-ryeong and Lee Sang-hyeon, "Letters from Maurice Courant and Three Portraits of the Scholar of Korean Studies: A Study on the Soul of a Young Scholar of Korean Studies Engraved in the PA-AP File of Collin de Plancy," *Yeolsang Journal of Classical Studies* 44 (2015): 87.

5) W.F. Sands, *Undiplomatic Memories* (Seoul: Jibmundang, 1999), 131.

6) Gustave-Charles-Marie Mutel (1854-1933)

7) Diaries Bishop Mutel kept for 42 years and five months from August 4, 1890, when he learned he was appointed to lead the Vicariate Apostolic in Korea, to December 31, 1932,

"The king has high hopes for France and desires a more capable French representative of higher position. The current representative is absolutely not up to the job and failed to earn his trust."

The second French minister to Korea and successor to Collin de Plancy was Hippolyte Frandin (1852-1926). He came to Korea in April 1892 but returned home due to his mother's death in March 1894, when Secretary Lefevre became a chargé d'affaires. Under these circumstances, Collin de Plancy returned as the third French minister and in the capacity of ambassador plenipotentiary. He arrived in Seoul in April 1896 and told King Gojong during his first audience to report his return, that "to help advance the interests of Korea for which I have great admiration, I put in a request with the French government to return to Korea. And here I am."[8]

During his second assignment in Korea, he put much effort in the construction of railways, managing to gain the right to lay the Seoul to Uiju line in 1896 and held a ground-breaking ceremony for the railway between Seoul and Gaeseong in 1902. These achievements

---

shortly before his death from illness on January 23, 1933. The diaries are massive records that cover his private life, church activities, reports by missionaries as well as the political, diplomatic and social problems of Joseon society. They are kept by the Paris Foreign Missions Society in Paris, France and have been translated and published in eight volumes by the Research Foundation for Korean Church History.

8) Entry in Bishop Mutel's diary, dated April 2, 1896.

amid the fierce rivalry with Russia and Japan were an important matter that deserves the interest of the home government. In the end, the construction was not completed by France but turned over to Japan. Still he endeavored to hire French technicians, and brought French people to various positions in administration, architecture, and teaching and got them into important roles in Korea.

It is known that he also helped modernize Korea's postal services. The Korean government's first attempt at modern postal services that resulted in establishment of the General Postal Administration (Ujeong Chongguk) in 1884 was frustrated due to the Gapsin Coup the same year. Its efforts continued and Collin de Plancy believed the education of postal personnel should be entrusted to foreigners, arranging for French officials to be employed in such positions. Such efforts enabled Korea to join the Universal Postal Union in 1900 and provide international postal services.[9] This led to increases in the volume of postcards sent and received. The number of postcards Collin de Plancy sent to his own family also increased from 1903. These postcards were donated to the Médiathèque du Grand Troyes in 1923.[10]

---

9) Orange, "Collin de Plancy and French Advisors," 97-98.
10) Orange, "Collin de Plancy and French Advisors," 182.

Collection of Korean cultural artifacts

From the early days of his placement in Korea, Collin de Plancy passionately collected a variety of Korean cultural artifacts like old books and ceramics.

To look for books to purchase, Collin de Plancy visited bookstores and temples here and there. His collection included popular literature written in Hangeul (the Korean alphabet), cult books, Buddhist books, and others rejected by intellectuals and the royal family.

His method of purchasing books can be known from *Voyage en Corée,* a travel log by a geographer named Charles Varat (1842-1893), who visited Korea while Collin de Plancy was there:

"A typical day in Seoul went like this: Mr. Collin de Plancy spread the rumor that a French traveller perched himself at the French legation every morning and was buying samples of every product made in this country. Merchants flocked around from early morning and my job was to carefully review their wares with an eye for Korean folklore. Any product from overseas was to be ruthlessly excluded. Fortunately Mr. Collin de Plancy placed his Korean secretaries, whom he taught French everyday, under my direction to help me sort things out. They explained those products about which I had no clue and bargained with merchants over the prices. Sometimes they called out enormous prices or turned down our proposals but there was no need to waste time arguing with them. They usually came back the next day and accepted the conditions we had offered the day before.

In the afternoon, we went around Seoul with French-speaking secretaries and bought up everything that held folklore value."[11]

Incapable of speaking Korean, he took the French-speaking personnel and toured the shops in Seoul. The assumption is that, thanks to this method and Collin de Plancy's discerning eye, he managed to quickly identify and purchase quality artifacts despite the brevity of his stay. Also thanks to his position as the highest French diplomat in Korea, Collin de Plancy received plenty of information on Korean books and received many as gifts. As a particular example, he received the Korean history *Dongguk-Tonggam* (東國通鑑) from Emperor Gojong.

He sent books he had purchased to his alma mater, L'École des Langues orientales, over three occasions: 1889, 1890, and 1891. Most of the graduates from the school became diplomats or interpreters and it was a kind of tradition to collect and send local books from different Eastern countries where they were stationed.

Collin de Plancy collected all manner of books, including religious

---

11) Daniel Bouchez, "Maurice Courant, the Pioneer of Korean Studies Part 1," trans. Jeon Su-yeon, *Journal of Korean Studies* 51 (1986): 157-158.

scriptures, creed books, classic novels, and *gasa* song texts. He collected clean books if possible, and if there were copper plates or wood blocks, he bought and provided quality paper to produce reprints. For this reason, his collection is still in good condition.

Those old books sent by Collin de Plancy made up the first collection of Korean books at L'École des Langues orientales. With this as a starter, the library of the school (presently the Institut National des Langues et Civilisations Orientales or National Institute for Oriental Languages and Civilizations) has come to retain 1,400 volumes of 630 old Korean books today. This is the largest collection of old Korean books in Europe.[12] The National Institute of History of Art (Institut National d'Histoire de l'Art) has two Korean old books, *Samgang Haengsildo* (*Conduct of the Three Fundamental Principles in Human Relationships*, 三綱行實圖) and *Jeonmun Cheonja* (篆文千字) while the National Library of France (Bibliothèque nationale de France) retains some 300 old Korean books and documents[13].

Collin de Plancy is known to have reserved a special affection for Korean ceramics. Since the 17th century, the French had greatly preferred Chinese ceramics and imported many items. Korean

---

12) Lee Jin-myeong, "State and Research Trends of Koreanology Materials in the Collections of the National Library of France and the National Institute for Oriental Languages and Civilizations," *Korean Studies* 2 (2003): 206-209.
13) Han Ji-hui, Kim Hyo-gyeong, and Lee Hye-eun, "Study of Rare Korean Books in the Collection of the National Library of France's Department of Manuscripts," *Bibliography Research* 69 (2017): 307-325.

ceramics were not introduced until the latter half of the 19th century. Collin de Plancy was enamored with the latter and donated his collection to the Musée national de Céramique (Sèvres) and many other museums and galleries.

Of them all, the Sèvres came to appreciate Korean ceramic culture thanks to Collin de Plancy and manufactured a variety of related products including European celadon. Collin de Plancy is regarded as the only French diplomat who cooperated in the collection and research of Korean ceramics during the modern transition period.

Collin de Plancy was also active in using ceramics for diplomatic purposes. Sadi Carnot (1837-1894), then French President, and Emperor Gojong gifted each other with ceramics from their respective countries to celebrate formal relations. First France sent ceramics from the Sèvres to Gojong in May 1888, and in return Gojong sent two pieces of Goryeo celadon. Active intervention by Collin de Plancy in this process can be confirmed in the following letter:

"The Joseon king sent various gifts to the French President, among which are two bowls inscribed with decorative lines and in excellent condition, and believed to have been produced in the 13th century. They are the best of their kind I have ever seen. When sending them to Paris, I recommended the Sèvres as a place to be entrusted with them. I believe President Carnot will willingly agree to you having them."[14]

Collin de Plancy also rendered active help to the establishment of a crafts school, a particular interest in modern Korea-France relations. He discovered Korea had difficulty producing ceramics and suggested as a solution the establishment of a special school for crafts and cooperation with Sèvres craftsmen. Things proceeded to discussing details with the Korean government but plans fell through due to budgetary issues. Nevertheless, the Ceramic Factory for Royal Use was established in 1901 with Sèvres craftsmen and state-of-the art facilities. A craftsman named Leopold Rémion came to Korea to demonstrate Western ceramic-making techniques while acquainting himself with Korean ceramics. However, this factory also closed down in 1904 due to financial issues. Collin de Plancy sought to reverse the shutdown, but to no avail due to a variety of reasons, including intervention by the Japanese government.

In addition, Collin de Plancy collected Buddhist and shamanistic paintings, old maps, furniture, and more, many of which are currently in the collection of the Musée national des Arts asiatiques-Guimet.

These activities by Collin de Plancy show us that he did more than just collect Korean cultural artifacts, also engaging in cultural

---

14) Eom Seung-hui, "Collection and Accommodation by the Musée national de Céramique (Sèvres) of Korean Ceramics during the Modern Times - Based on the Collection in 2015," *Journal of Korean Modern and Contemporary Art History* 29 (2015): 266.

cooperation between Korea and France quite actively during his placement here. This is why Victor Collin de Plancy is remembered up to the present day as the most significant contributor to exposing Europe to Korean culture.

Jikji in the Collin de Plancy Collection

The most famous among the Korean artifacts collected by Collin de Plancy is the second volume of *Baegun Hwasang Chorok Buljo Jikji Simche Yojeol* (白雲和尙抄錄佛祖直指心體要節). Commonly referred to as *Jikji* as an abbreviation or as written on its cover, it was printed with movable metal type at the Heungdeoksa temple in Cheongju, Korea in 1377 and is the world's oldest extant book printed with movable metal type.

Jikji was on display at the Korean Pavilion of the 1900 Paris Exposition and was introduced in Maurice Courant's *Bibliographie Coréenne*. It began to gain attention when it was presented at a book fair held by the National Library of France in 1972, the first International Book Year designated by UNESCO. In September 2001, *Jikji* was included on UNESCO's Memory of the World Register and is currently retained by the National Library of France's Department of Manuscripts (Départment des Manuscrits) as book no. 109 of its Korean collection.

Let us go back to 1900 and look at the Paris Exposition, which the French government held for seven months from April to celebrate the previous century and leap into the next century. With participation from many entities from around the world, it featured a wide range of advanced machinery, inventions, films, etc. that had come out since the Industrial Revolution and attracted 50 million visitors.

Photo 3: Jikji

In 1897, three years prior, Gojong, responding to the situation at home and abroad, established the Korean Empire and declared it to the rest of the world as an independent, sovereign state. Collin de Plancy actively recommended that Korea participate in the exhibition as an opportunity to publicize existence of the Korean Empire to the international community.

According to *Souvenir de Séoul*, the publicity booklet for Korea, the Korean Pavilion was built as a two-story *hanok* building in a quiet place by Suffren Road in the Champ-de-Mars square in Paris. It introduced Minister Collin de Plancy as its promoter. Gojong sent Min Yeong-chan (1874~1948) as a minister to six European nations and it is valuable in terms of both history and Korean linguistics as it evidences use of Hangeul in the 19th century. It is interesting that the book was part of the Collin de Plancy collection considering that Korea-France diplomatic relations began with the French campaign against Korea in retaliation for the execution of French Catholic missionaries. As with *Byeonghaktong*, *Cheoksa Yuneum* is also pasted with a Collin de Plancy bookplate.

Also featured are *Goryeo ji Myeonyeong* (高麗之面影), illustrations of Mt. Bukhansan, Mt. Namsan, high-ranking officials and commoners, courtesans, shops and streets in Seoul as of October 1905; and *Korean Architecture Survey Report* (韓國建築調查報告) published in 1904 by Tokyo Imperial University's Engineering College. The latter was a report of surveys of Korean architecture in Gyeonggi-do Province (with a focus on Seoul), Hwanghae-do, and Gyeongsang-do (with a focus on Busan) from July to September 1902 by Sekino Tadashi (關野貞, 1867-1935), a professor from the college. They are thought to be among the last items Collin de Plancy collected.

Also interesting are postcards exchanged between Collin de Plancy and his family in Paris. These postcards feature landscapes and buildings as well as people in Paris, France, Egypt and other countries of North Africa, those on the Arabian Peninsula, India, kingdoms and countries on the Indochina Peninsula, Korea, China, and Japan.

Not a few among them are believed to have been written to his mother in Paris from Korea. They were produced by commercial and as Korean representative at the fair. However, it was Collin de Plancy who carried the most weight: he took a leave from 1899 to 1900 to stay in France and prepare for the Korean Pavilion. Later he was awarded the first *hun* rank and a Taegeuk insignia by Gojong for his service in this regard.

Photo 4: Inside the Korean Pavilion at the Paris Exposition

The Korean Pavilion showcased a variety of furniture, farm implements and produce, musical instruments, jewelry, clothing, hunting tools, weaponry, etc., sent by the Korean government, as well as ceramics, books, and coins owned by Collin de Plancy.[15]

The *Bulletin of the Archaeological, Historical & Artistic Society: Old Paper* (*Bulletin de la Société archéologique, historique & artistique: le Vieux papier*), published in 1900, carried an article entitled "Korea's Old Paper (Vieux Papiers de Corée)," which deals with Korea's paper and printing culture and introduces *Jikji* as presented at the Paris Exposition's Korean Pavilion:

Almost two centuries before Gutenberg invented printing in Europe, Koreans were already printing with movable type. To the eyes of the visitor, the oldest among the exhibits is the one in the Collin de Plancy collection. This is a book that has the title of a Buddhist doctrine book and comes in octavo format. Written by Baegun, a monk, the last page has the following indication: Printed at the Heungdeoksa temple on the outskirts of Cheongju in 1377, the seventh year of Seongwang(宣光).

(Presque deux siècles avant que Gutenberg eût inventé l'imprimerie en Europe, les Coréens imprimaient déjà à l'aide de caractères mobiles....Le plus ancien connu est exposé, sous les yeux du visiteur, dans la vitrine de M. Collin de Plancy. C'est un livre intitulé : *Traits édifiants des Patriarches* rassemblés par le bonze Pack-Oun, un volume in-8°, portant a la dernière page l'indication suivante : En

---

15) Liste D'objets Exposes Lors de L'exposition Unniverselle de 1900 A Paris, Archives Nationales F-12-4224~4357.

1377, 7e année de SinanBoang, à la Bonzerie de Heung-Tek, hors du chef-lieu du district de Tchyeng-Tijou.)[16]

   As it explains that printing with movable metal type had begun in Korea rather than by Gutenberg in Germany; the indication on the last page of *Jikji*, owned by Collin de Plancy, says that it was printed with movable metal type at the Heungdeoksa temple in 1377; and it was the oldest exhibit at the exposition, the value of *Jikji* must have already been known and publicized through the 1900 exposition.

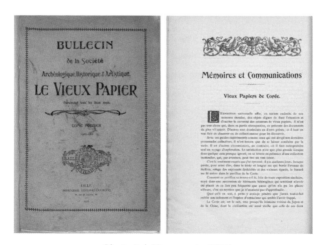

Photo 5: *le Vieux papier,* 1900

---

16) VIVAREZ, HENRY, Vieux Papiers de Corée, *Bulletin de la Société archéologique, historique & artistique le Vieux papier,* 1900, p. 79.

Collin de Plancy was unfamiliar with Korean but could understand Korean books and documents written in Chinese characters. This enabled him to appreciate the value of Korea's books and book culture. In fact, he wrote on the cover and inner cover of *Jikji* himself, "The oldest known Korean book printed with metal type, with date=1377 (Le plus ancien livre coréen imprimé connu en caractères fondus, avec date=1377)" and "Buddhist doctrine. Printed using metal type at the Heungdeoksa temple in 1377. The oldest printed Korean book known (Traits edifiant des Patriarches. En 1377, a la bonzerie de Heung Tuk imprime a l'aide de caracteres fondus. Le plus ancien livre coréen imprime connu)."

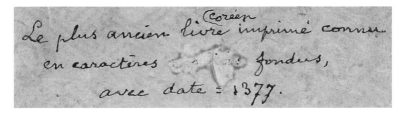

Photo 6: Indication on *Jikji*

He pasted a bookplate where "葛" of his Chinese-character name "葛林德" and "EX LIBRIS COLLIN DE PLANCY" are indicated on the inner cover. He did so with all the books he collected to clarify his ownership.

Photo 7: Collin de Plancy bookplate

A book that must be mentioned together with *Jikji* is Maurice Courant's *Bibliographie Coréenne* (*Korean Bibliography*). Consisting of four volumes, the book is an indispensible reference for any researcher of Korean studies in terms of both form and content.

Maurice Courant arrived in Korea as an interpreter for the French legation in May 1890. He also went to L'École des Langues orientales as Collin de Plancy did and majored in Chinese and Japanese. Not familiar with Korea, Courant did not find Korea interesting at first. Collin de Plancy showed his collection of Korean books to Courant and proposed that they catalog all the books published in Korea together. Courant wrote in the Introduction to *Bibliographie Coréenne* published in 1894:

> "I would like to make clear that due credit should be given to Mr. Collin de Plancy, the French minister to Korea at the time this project was undertaken. It was he who came up with the idea of writing this catalog in the first place and he provided many accurate pieces of information and excellent advice on numerous occasions."[17]

The writing of the bibliography continued even after Collin de Plancy left Korea in June 1891 for a new post in Tokyo, and Courant

---

17) Lee Hui-jae, *Bibliographie Coréenne - Revised and Translated* (original work by Maurice Courant) (Seoul: Ilchokak, 1994), xi-xii.

in March 1892 for his new post in China. Courant also wrote in the Introduction, "I searched every bookstore in Seoul and looked through every book they had. I bought books that seemed most interesting and made detailed notes about the others." Even on leave, Courant visited different places in Europe that held relevant materials. In *Bibliographie Coréenne*, Courant put down acronyms of locations for each item when it became known to him: these include B.R. (Seoul's Kyujanggak library); Bibl. Nat. (Bibliothèque nationale de France or National Library of France); Brit. M. (British Museum's Department of East Asia); C. des Int. (Seoul's Sayeogwon Office of Interpreters); Com. F. S. (Seoul's French legation); L.O.V. (library of L'École des Langues orientales in Paris); and Miss. étr. Séoul (library of Seoul's Paris Foreign Missions Society). Individual collections include A.V. (A. Vissière), C.P. (Collin de Plancy), J.B. (J. Beauvais), M.C. (Maurice Courant), Coll. v. d. Gabelentz (Collection of von de Gabelentz), and Coll. Varat (Collection of Varat).

While in Seoul, Courant asked L'École des Langues orientales, their alma mater, to publish *Bibliographie Coréenne*, which the school decided to do as part of the Publications de L'Ecole des Langues Orientales and under co-authorship of Collin de Plancy and Courant. However, in early 1892, while in Japan Collin de Plancy wrote to Courant that his contribution to the writing was so insignificant that Courant should be the sole author of the book.[18] Courant's reply to

---

18) Bouchez, "Maurice Courant, the Pioneer of Korean Studies Part 1," 160.

this, left in the PA-AP (Papiers d'agents-Archives privées) file of Collin de Plancy at the French Ministry of Europe and Foreign Affairs goes like this:

> "I am sorry to disagree with you, but who came up with the idea for this book in the first place? Was it I who thought to look into and study Korean books and rummage the shelves at bookstores? Don't you remember I objected at first? It took you several months to persuade me join you in the project and I took it only to satisfy you. I took interest in the project only afterwards [...] You are saying you did nothing! From the initial concept, draft for execution, bibliographic approach to how to proceed and the writing format to writing of annotations for five or six pages, you ended up writing one volume's worth, which corresponds to a third of the book."[19]

Courant stayed in Joseon only one year and ten months (May 1890 to March 1892) before leaving for China. However, he continued to work on *Bibliographie Coréenne* outside Korea. As a result, Vol. 1 came out in 1894, followed by Vol. 2 in 1895 and Vol. 3 in 1896. Continuous revisions were made until a supplement was added in

---

19) Pusan National University Institute of Humanities Research et. al., eds., *Soul of a Young Scholar of Korean Studies Engraved in the Collin de Plancy File* (2017), 246-247 (letter dated Feb. 25, 1982).

1901. There are 3,821 books, categorized in nine parts: education, studies of languages, Confucianism, literature, manners and customs, history and geography, sciences and arts, religion, and external relations. This categorization is Courant's own work.

Of particular note is that the 1901 supplement to *Bibliographie Coréenne* lists *Jikji* as no. 3738. Recorded is that it is one book, and only volume 2 of two volumes, and is a large octavo in size. It is marked with "C.P.," meaning it belonged to the Collin de Plancy collection. Added is the following annotation:

> The following is written on the last page of the book: "Printed with cast metal type at the Heungdeoksa temple on the outskirts of Cheongju in 1377. If this record is correct, this cast

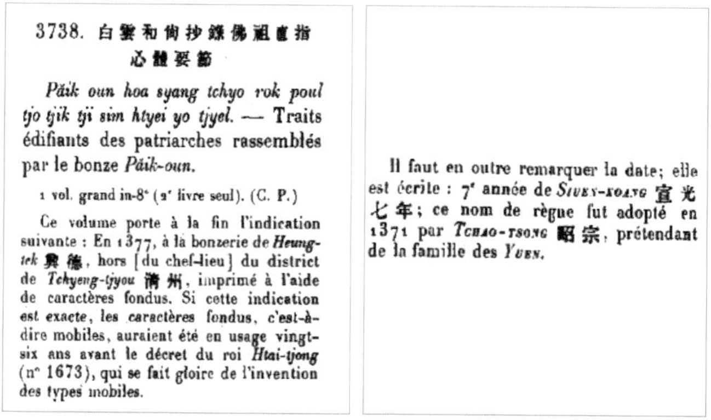

3738. 白雲和尙抄錄佛祖直指心體要節

Păik oun hoa syang tchyo rok poul tjo tjik tji sim htyei yo tjyel. — Traits édifiants des patriarches rassemblés par le bonze *Păik-oun.*

1 vol. grand in-8° (2e livre seul). (C. P.)

Ce volume porte à la fin l'indication suivante : En 1377, à la bonzerie de *Heung-tek* 興德, hors [du chef-lieu] du district de *Tchyeng-tjyou* 淸州, imprimé à l'aide de caractères fondus. Si cette indication est exacte, les caractères fondus, c'est-à-dire mobiles, auraient été en usage vingt-six ans avant le décret du roi *Htai-tjong* (n° 1673), qui se fait gloire de l'invention des types mobiles.

Il faut en outre remarquer la date; elle est écrite : 7e année de *Siuen-koang* 宣光七年; ce nom de règne fut adopté en 1371 par *Tchao-tsong* 昭宗, prétendant de la famille des *Yuen.*

Photo 8: The section of *Bibliographie Coréenne* on *Jikji*

type was used some 26 years ago before the order of Taejong (n°1673). Taejong is Joseon's third king and one of the achievements claimed during his reign is the invention of type. The "seventh year of Seongwang" is also noteworthy. Seongwang is the era name Xuanguang (1371-1378) adopted by Emperor Zhaozong of the Northen Yuan dynasty who claimed to inherit the Yuan dynasty in 1371.

Collin de Plancy and Courant clearly knew that Korea's metal type printing preceded not only Germany's Gutenberg but also China. In the extended Introduction to *Bibliographie Coréenne* Vol. 1, Courant wrote, "In terms of printing technology, Korea outdid China and preceded Europe. In 1403, Taejong, the third king of Joseon, ordered casting of type in bronze."[20] Also, *Juja Sasil* (鑄字事實) was listed as no. 1673 in *Bibliographie Coréenne*. Published in 1858, this book records the history of metal casting of type throughout the Joseon dynasty, including the casting of eight kinds of *gyemi* type (100,000 sorts), *gyeongja* type, *gabin* type, *imjin* type, *jeongyu* type, *imin* type, *saengsaeng* type, and *jeongni* type.

At the beginning of the annotation for *Juja Sasil*, Courant copied the postscripts of *Munheon Bigo* (文獻備考), published in 1770:

---

20) Lee, *Bibliographie Coréenne - Revised and Translated*, 11-12.

"In the third year of his reign and year of gyemi (1403), Taejong gave the following order: Though knowledge of books should be spread to facilitate the rule of the nation, we are located east across the sea and therefore Chinese books are hard to come by. Wood blocks are easily worn out and it is difficult to engrave each and every book. Thus, I intend to have types cast in bronze and books printed with them to spread their existence."[21]

The assumption is that Courant did not know about the records on metal type printing during Goryeo, the dynasty before Joseon. For instance, Lee Gyu-bo's *Dongguk Isang Gukjip* (東國李相國集) from that period records that 28 copies of *Sangjeong Gogeum Yemun* (詳定古今禮文) were printed with cast type and distributed to government offices. Another Goryeo record about metal type printing is *Nammyeongcheon Hwasang Songjeungdoga* (南明泉和尙頌證道歌). For this reason, Courant determined metal type printing was invented in Korea in the third year of Taejong's reign, namely 1403, based on the records of *Juja Sasil* and *Munheon Bigo*, and probably not completely sure that *Jikji* was printed with metal type in Cheongju, far from the capital during the Goryeo period 26 years prior, used the expression, "If this record is correct." Nevertheless, Collin de Plancy was sure that

---

21) Lee, *Bibliographie Coréenne - Revised and Translated*, 411.

Jikji was "The oldest known Korean book printed with metal type." In consideration of the writing and publication process of *Bibliographie Coréenne*; display at the Paris Exposition; and *Jikji* being listed not in the *Bibliographie Coréenne* volumes published between 1894 and 1896, but in the 1901 supplement, it is believed that Collin de Plancy got hold of *Jikji* between 1896 and 1899.

The Victor Collin de Plancy collection

From March 27 to 30, 1911, the collection of Collin de Plancy was put up for auction at Hôtel Drouot, an auction house in Paris. The auction catalog, *Collection of an Amateur, Works of Art from Korea,*

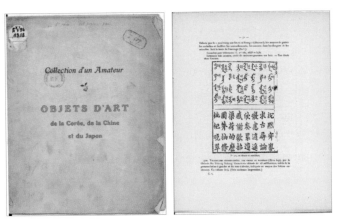

Photo 9: *Collection of an Amateur (Collection d'un amateur)*

China, and Japan (*Collection d'un amateur, objets d'art de la Corée, de la Chine et du Japon*),[22] issued before the auction, included 883 items Collin de Plancy had collected from the three Asian countries.

Of these, 700 had come from Korea, including books, maps, rubbings, portraits, lacquerware, folding screens, furniture, coins, and more. Korean books were listed as auction items no. 711 to 798 on pages 66 to 85 on the catalog. This catalog carried one image each from no. 714 *Iryun Haengsildo* (二倫行實圖), no. 717 *Cheonjamun* (千字文), and no. 719 *Jineonjip* (眞言集),[23] and three images from no. 713 *Samgang Haengsildo* (三綱行實圖) to draw attention from auction participants. *Jikji* was given auction item no. 711, the first of the Korean items, and the explanation added that "this book was printed with metal type at the Heungdeoksa temple in Cheongju, Korea in 1377: the earliest among books printed with metal type." However, the book sold for the highest price was no. 713 *Samgang Haengsildo,* to an individual with the family name Vigne for 3,000 francs. It was later owned by Jacques Doucet before donation to the Institut National d'Histoire de l'Art. In the meantime, *Jikji* was sold to a jeweler in Paris, named Henry Vever for a relatively low price of 180 francs. The National Library of France bought a total of 72 books at the auction, but not *Jikji*. The library might have thought its value indicated on the catalog

22) Hotel Drouot, *Collection d'un amateur: Objets d'art de la corée, de la Chine et du Japon, 27-30 mars 1911,* Paris: Hotel Drouot, 1911.
23) Its original name is *Buljeongsim Daranigyeong* (佛頂心陀羅尼經).

was exaggerated. Fortunately, Henry Vever's grandson, François Mautin, donated the book to the National Library of France in August 1950, in keeping with the grandfather's will. *Jikji*, currently in the collection of the national library, has a bookplate pasted inside that says it was owned in Paris from 1911 to 1943 and thereby represents part of Henry Vever's collection. It is thought that Collin de Plancy, who retired from official life in 1907, returned to Paris and put his collection to order.

Archives that offer a sneak peek into the private life of Victor Collin de Plancy are housed by the Médiathèque du Grand Troyes. This collection includes 175 writings, images, *objet*, and more.[24]

First are his dissertation for a law degree in 1877 and papers on reptiles, amphibians, and zoology.

We mainly remember him as a collector but he was also a scholar complete with academic qualities. He authored such papers as "Catalog of Reptiles and Batrachians Inhabiting the Aube River and Study on the Geographical Distribution of Reptiles and Batrachians in Eastern France (Catalogue des Reptiles et Batraciens du département de l'Aube et Etude sur la distribution géographique des Reptiles et Batraciens de l'Est de la France)" carried in the *Bulletin of the Historical and Natural Science Society of Semur (Bulletin de la*

---

24) Berquet, François, Le Fonds Collin de Plancy à la Médiathèque du Grand Troyes, *Roman d'un voyageur : Victor Collin de Plancy, l'histoire des collections coréennes en France*, Cité de la céramique Sèvres et Limoges, 2015. p. 72.

Société des sciences historiques et naturelles de Semur) in 1877; and "Mating and Spawning of Lizards in France (L'accouplement et la ponte chez les Lézards de France)" and "Note on Parasitic Dipteran Insects of Amphibians (Note sur les insectes diptères parasites des batraciensles)" in the *Bulletin of the Zoological Society of France, Paris* (*Bulletin de la Société zoologique de France, Paris*) in 1877. In 1879, he translated *Archaeological and Historical Research on Beijing* (*Recherches archéologiques et historiques sur Pékin*) written by Emil Bretschneider, which L'École des Langues orientales published.

Photo 10: *Bulletin of the Historical and Natural Science Society of Semur*, 1877

Except for three novels by Emile Zola and Pierre Loti and one fable by Jean de la Fontaine, this collection mainly consists of reference books. There are dozens of writings on law, diplomacy and the modern diplomatic world; books on medical science for the general public; and yearbooks. Also included is a 37.5×50.5 cm map on the 1900 Paris Exposition.

Also important from this collection are items on Far Eastern Asian languages, history, arts, and culture. Collin de Plancy bound together French and other foreign magazines, brochures, programs, and separate editions on these topics into eight volumes. There are also scrapbooks of newspaper articles on Far Eastern Asia's economic and political events from 1884 to 1922. He collected these as references for his diplomatic work.

There are also 91 documents in French and English on China, Korea, and Japan, with dozens of them about learning and practicing Chinese and Korean. Also included are grammar books and dictionaries such as the "French-Latin-Chinese Dictionary" by Paul Fernie (1869-1872), the "Small French-Korean Dictionary (Petit Dictionnaire Français-Coréen)" (1901) by Charles Alévêque, and "Korean Grammar" and "Korean-French Dictionary" by the Corean Mission (1880, 1881).

This collection also includes 41 old Chinese, Korean and Japanese books from the 18th to 19th centuries.[25] An example of the old Korean

---

25) Lee Hye-eun and Lee Eun-ryeong, *Preliminary Research on the Collin de Plancy Collection: With a Focus on Materials in France's Médiathèque du Grand Troyes* (Seoul: Overseas Korean Cultural Heritage Foundation, 2016).

books is *Byeonghaktong* (兵學通) printed with wood blocks in 1785. On the order of King Jeongjo in the first year of his reign (1776), Jang Ji-hang, the law enforcement minister and Royal Guards officer, compiled this military training manual.

Another example is *Yujungoe Daesominindeung Cheoksa Yuneum* (諭中外大小民人等斥邪綸音) printed with *imjin* metal type in 1893. This item is special because it is a royal message promulgated after the Catholic Persecution of 1839, also known as the Gihae Persecution, in the fifth year of King Heonjong's reign. Aimed at the public, this message condemns Catholicism and extols neo-Confucianism, Joseon's dominant philosophy. As the religion had been already widely propagated through society, including among the disadvantaged, it was first written in Chinese characters and again in Hangeul for the common people to read. It first explains the background to promulgation of the message. It looks at the origin of neo-Confucianism, upright learning, and historically criticizes Catholicism by citing its introduction by Lee Seong-hun in 1784, the Catholic Persecution of 1801 (Sinyu Persecution), and the Hwang Sa-yeong Incident in 1810. Almost 40 years after the Sinyu Persecution, the "unwholesome and vicious" religion was thriving even more. With this background explained, it goes on to refute Catholic doctrines in detail including its respect for the heavens and the Resurrection of Christ. Lastly, it conciliates Catholics as they are also the nation's people and the king's legitimate children. The title written on the cover is *Cheoksa Yuneum* (斥邪綸音)

photo studios in Seoul that catered to Westerners and Japanese and feature photos of then famous spots and landscapes, including Jemulpo Port, Namdaemun Gate, a boat on the Hangang River, a panoramic view of Seoul, Gwanghwamun Gate, the Geunjeongjeon throne hall of the Gyeongbokgung Palace, Songdo, Suwon, Busan, the French legation, Mt. Bukhansan, and the opening ceremony of the Seoul to Busan railway. Most bear dates and scribbles or titles and deliver news about how he was doing. They are valuable for research on the history of such places.

Photo 11: Postcard from Victor Collin de Plancy (Médiathèque du Grand Troyes)

There are also photo albums. Two contain photos taken in China in 1883 and of a mine in Korea, the latter photos including the mine office and surroundings. The third album consists of some 100 photos of Collin de Plancy, other foreigners in Korea, and French diplomats. The photos of Collin de Plancy were taken in many places such as Shanghai, Tokyo, and Siam. Two black frames marked CP 678 and CP 679 picture his father, Jacques, and his mother, each with two young sons. They were taken in 1860 and 1853, respectively.

Photo 12: Photo album (Médiathèque du Grand Troyes)

Photo 13: "Gal Rim-deok (葛林德)" seal

The collection also includes several wood carvings, with one example being a seal engraved with "葛林德" (Korean pronunciation: Gal Rim-deok), Collin de Plancy's Chinese name. Measuring 12.9 × 4.3 cm, this wooden seal looks to be the same font as "葛" affixed on the Victor Collin de Plancy bookplates. But the imprint of the seal 葛林德 has not be found on any of books in the Collin de Plancy collection.

This collection also includes his several certificates of degrees, medals he received during his period of service, and credentials received from the French government for a minister and minister plenipotentiary in Seoul.

There are also decorations conferred by the Korean emperor, including a silver metal celebrating the 50th birthday of the Korean emperor (comméniratuve de la 50e année de l'empereur de Corée décrenée à Collin de Plancy, ministre de la République), received on September 7, 1901; a first-class Order of the Taegeuk (Premiére classe de l'ordre la de Htai-keuk (T'aegŭk) décrenéé par l'empereur de Corée à Collin de Plancy, ministre plénipotentiaire de France), received on October 20, 1902; and a Grand Cross of the Order of the Plum Flower (Grand-croix de l'ordre la Fluer de prunier décrenéé par l'empereur de Corée au ministre plénipotentiaire de France), received on November 15, 1906.

The last of Victor Collin de Plancy

Almost nothing is known about the private life of Victor Collin de Plancy, but there is an unofficial tragic love story between him and a Korean dancer from the royal court. The story even inspired a novel. However, the official record in France is that he never married and left no direct descendents.

Collin de Plancy died at his home at 10 Square du Croisic, Paris in 1922 and a funeral was conducted at the St. François-Xavie church at 9 am on Saturday, October 28. As mentioned above, he spent 27 years of his 30-year diplomatic career in Asia, with 13 of those in Korea. His passionate interest in and study of Asian culture, and in particular, Korean culture helped make Korea, a largely-unknown country then, known to France. This ceaselessly occurred throughout his life.

Bibliography

Bouchez, Daniel. "Maurice Courant, the Pioneer of Korean Studies Part 1." *Journal of Korean Studies* 51 (1986): 153-194.

Bouchez, Daniel. "Maurice Courant, the Pioneer of Korean Studies Part 2." *Journal of Korean Studies* 52 (1986): 83-121.

Courant, Maurice. *Bibliographie Coréenne.* Paris: E. Leroux, 1894~1896, 1901.

Eom, Seung-hui. "Collection and Accommodation by the Musée national de Céramique (Sèvres) of Korean Ceramics during the Modern Times – Based on the Collection in 2015." *Journal of Korean Modern and Contemporary Art History* 29 (2015): 261-286.

François Roudant, Le fonds collin de plancy – Dé posé à la bibliothèque municipale de troyes, Genève: Edition Slatkine, 1994.

French School of the Far East and Korea University Museum. *Memory of Seoul: Korea and France, 1886-1905.* 2006.

Han, Ji-hui, Kim, Hyo-gyeong, and Lee, Hye-eun. "Study of Rare Korean Books in the Collection of the National Library of France's Department of Manuscripts." *Bibliography Research* 69 (2017): 307-325.

Hotel Drouot. *Collection d'un amateur: Objets d'art de la corée, de la Chine et du Japon, 27-30 mars 1911*, Paris: Hotel Drouot, 1911.

Hwang, Jeong-ha. "Publication of *Jikji* and Account of Its Transmission to This Day." *History and Silhak* 35 (2008): 37-88.

Lee, Eun-ryeong and Lee, Sang-hyeon. "Letters from Maurice Courant and Three Portraits of the Scholar of Korean Studies: A Study on the Soul of a Young Scholar of Korean Studies Engraved in the PA-AP File of Collin de Plancy."

Lee Hui-jae. *Bibliographie Coréenne - Revised and Translated* (original work by Maurice Courant). Seoul: Ilchokak, 1994.

Lee, Hui-jae. "Essay on Maurice Courant and *Bibliographie Coréenne.*" *Sookmyung Women's University Collection of Dissertations* 28 (Seoul: Sookmyung Women's University Dissertation Editorial Committee, 1988): 325-364.

Lee, Hui-jae. "State of Old Korean Books Located in France and Development Directions." *Results of and Tasks for Collection of Old Korean Writings Overseas* (Seoul: National Library of Korea, 2011): 27-46.

Lee, Hye-eun and Lee, Hui-jae. "Status of and Possible Ways to Use Old Korean Book in the Collection of the Collège de France." *Journal of the Korean Society for Library and*

Information Science 45 (4) (2011): 235-251.

Lee, Hye-eun and Lee, Eun-ryeong. *Preliminary Research on the Collin de Plancy Collection: With a Focus on Materials in France's Médiathèque du Grand Troyes*. Seoul: Overseas Korean Cultural Heritage Foundation, 2016.

Lee, Hye-eun. "Another *Bibliographie Coréenne*: Oreste Toutzevitch Note." *Cogito* 82 (2017): 450-477.

Lee, Hye-eun. "A Historical Approach to the Recognition and Research of Maurice Courant and *Bibliographie Coréenne*." *Cogito* 86 (2018): 39-68.

Lee, Jin-myeong. "State and Research Trends of Koreanology Materials in the Collections of the National Library of France and National Institute for Oriental Languages and Civilizations." *Korean Studies* 2 (2003): 183-221.

Roman d'un voyageur: Victor Collin de Plancy, l'histoire des collections coréennes en France, Cité de la céramique Sèvres et Limoges, 2015.

Pusan National University Institute of Humanities Research, Jeom Pil-jae Institute, and Collège de France Institute of Korean Studies Library, eds. *Soul of a Young Scholar of Korean Studies Engraved in the Collin de Plancy File*. Seoul: Somyung Books, 2017.

Sands, W.F. *Undiplomatic Memories*. Seoul: Jibmundang, 1999.

Vivarez, Henry. Vieux Papiers de Corée, *Bulletin de la Société archéologique, historique & artistique le Vieux papier,* 1900.

Yeolsang Journal of Classical Studies 44 (2015): 75-141.

Maurice Courant and *Bibliographie Coréenne*

Lee Hye-Eun

Sookmyung Women's University

Maurice Courant and *Bibliographie Coréenne*

The most notable publication about Korea in any reference rooms in European and North American libraries that retain publications on East Asia is definitely *Bibliographie Coréenne* (*Korean Bibliography*) by Maurice Courant (1865-1935). *Bibliographie Coréenne* is a bibliography that lists materials collected and researched by Courant in the one year and ten months from May 1890 to March 1892 while he served as a secretary at the French legation in Seoul; those retained by Victor Collin de Plancy (1853-1922), then French minister to Korea, the French Bishop Gustave Mutel (1854-1933), and other individuals; and old publications held by the British Museum, Japan's Imperial Library in Ueno, Korea's Kyujanggak (the royal library of the Joseon Dynasty), etc. The bibliography is in nine parts, and covers a total 3,821 books in 36 chapters. Its Introduction is so rich in information that it alone has been translated and published separately on several occasions. It is an academic record of Korea's books, characters, philosophies, and literary works at the end of the 19th century, and is based on Korean publications. In a situation when there were insufficient materials in Western languages about Korea's books and literary culture, the content and significance of Courant's *Bibliographie Coréenne* have been introduced through a variety of channels since the first volume was published in 1894. The bibliography is particularly known for its decisive role in revealing the value of *Baegun Hwasang Chorok Buljo Jikji Simche Yojeol* (白雲和尙抄錄佛祖直指心體要節), recognized as the world's oldest surviving book printed with movable metal type, thereby helping to confirm its great importance in the world's history of printing. This article looks at who Maurice Courant, called the "pioneer of Korean studies," was and the contributions he left as a scholar to Koreanology. It also intends to shed new light on the value of *Bibliographie Coréenne*.

The life[1] and studies of Maurice Courant

Maurice Courant was born on October 12, 1865 in Paris as the first son of Charles Isidore Courant (1826-1888) from Normandy, and Marie Cosnard (1835-1907) from Paris. He passed the baccalauréat in 1883 and entered the law school of the University of Paris the same year and earned a bachelor's degree in 1886. In 1885, he enrolled with L´Ecole des Langues

---

1) The most comprehensive and detailed study on the life of Maurice Courant so far is: Daniel Bouchez, "Maurice Courant," *Journal asiatique*, Tome CCLXXI (1983): 43-150. A translation of this paper by Jeon Su-yeon can be found on pp. 153-194 and 83-121 of the *Journal of Korean Studies* (No. 51-52, Jun.-Sept.) issued by the Institute of Korean Studies of Yonsei University. This paper is regarded as the most important on Courant and was included in another paper, *Soul of a Young Scholar of Korean Studies Engraved in the Collin de Plancy File* (file at the PA-AP that contains documents related to Collin de Plancy) published in 2017. The life of Maurice Courant as introduced in this paper the reader holds is based on that document.

Orientales Vivantes and studied Chinese and Japanese, and in 1888, received a diplôme. He was then dispatched to the French legation in China's Peking as a trainee interpreter, which was the start of his career as a translator for the French Ministry of European and Foreign Affairs. He stayed in China for 21 months, during the last six of which he is known to have worked as chief interpreter in place of Arnold Vissière. Also during this period, Courant conducted a study, "The Court in Peking (La Cour de Péking)," which earned him an interpreter award from the Ministry in 1891.

On May 23, 1890, Courant was attached to Seoul as a secretary interpreter, succeeding Francois Guérin at 25. The French minister to Korea then was Collin de Plancy, who was also a graduate from L´Ecole des Langues Orientales Vivantes and had a great interest in Eastern culture and arts. Courant did not want to come to Seoul and looked for the opportunity to go elsewhere, likely because he had studied Chinese and Japanese, not Korean. Collin de Plancy showed Courant Korean books he had collected to spark an interest in the younger man in Korean culture. Collin de Plancy even suggested that Courant join him in listing up Korean publications. As Courant wrote in his Introduction to *Bibliographie Coréenne*, he visited bookstores in Seoul and became an enthusiastic collector and student of the information therein. With his knowledge of Chinese, Courant was able to understand Korean books as well, mostly written in Chinese characters as they were.

Photo 1: Maurice Courant   Photo 2: *Bibliographie Coréenne*

During my two-year stay in Seoul, out of my curiosity about all these books about which almost no information could be gained from European publications or other foreign residents, I first started studying books Mr. Collin de Plancy, the French minister to Korea, once owned and later donated to the L´Ecole des Langues Orientales library. This first study became a hobby, and encouraged by my superior's kind advice, I continued my research. I searched every bookstore in Seoul and looked through every book they had. I bought those that seemed most interesting and made detailed notes about the others. I was also greatly helped by other foreign residents who provided the greatest favor of showing books they had for my reference. The Koreans did not easily respond to my requests but a few provided very rare books. Thanks to all of this, I came to know of numerous books, some of which are very rare and cannot be found anywhere else.[2]

Though he did not start the research of his own volition, it seems that Courant went ahead with it with great enthusiasm, immersing himself in it even during his leaves.

During my holidays back in Europe, I visited many places that have important Korean materials. In Paris, I went to see those at the National Library of France Admiral Roze brought with him in 1866 from his expedition; Mr. Varat's 1888 collection, presently at the Guimet Museum; and those at L'Ecole des Langues Orientales I studied in Seoul before they were sent to Paris as I mentioned earlier. In London, I was able to scrutinize important books at the British Museum. In particular, I was greatly assisted by the two librarians at the National Library of France, Mr. Deprez and Mr. Feer as well as their counterpart at the British Museum, Mr. R.K. Douglas, who provided great convenience that I could go through the books under their care. I am enormously grateful to Mr. G.

---

2) Lee Hui-jae, *Bibliographie Coréenne - Revised and Translated* (韓國書誌: 修正飜譯版) (original work by Maurice Courant) (Seoul: Ilchokak, 1994), 4.

von der Gabelentz for giving the list of his collection of books. Unfortunately, I was never able to get the list of Korean materials from Saint Petersburg, which had not yet been classified. Lastly, in Tokyo, whether it was at bookstores, at Zojoji Temple (増上寺), or at the Imperial Library in Ueno, I was able to find many interesting books unavailable in Korea.[3]

Collin de Plancy, who had suggested this project in the first place, was transferred to Peking in June 1891, but returned to Seoul in 1895 as consul general and full minister and stayed until 1906. Courant left Korea in March 1892 after 21 months of sojourn but did not give up on the project. He continued with his research and received essential assistance in the form of materials from Bishop Mutel and others who remained in Korea.

During his time in Korea he wrote *Historical Repertoire of Korean Administration (Répertoire historique de l'administration coréenne)* in 1891, which earned him a diplomat award in 1892. In late 1891, *Le tableau de la littéraire coréenne* was chosen as the title of what was to be *Bibliographie Coréenne* in the end, and was planned to be published by Paris' Ernest Leroux as part of the *Publications of L´Ecole des Langues Orientales*. However, in early 1892, Collin de Plancy wrote a letter in which he explained that he had invited Courant to join the project in the hope that it would ignite his interest in the country of their sojourn, and suggested

3) Ibid., 5.

that Courant list himself as the sole author, as Collin de Plancy's contribution to the work was so insignificant. By then, the sections on administration, rites, Buddhism, and Taoism had been completed and what remained were sections on history books and anthologies. For the first part, Courant was to use existing lists rather than going through actual books and the second part was to take more time as it required research on individual authors.

Back in Paris in October 1892, Courant married Hélène Schefer, a daughter of the L´Ecole des Langues Orientales' dean, on January 30, 1893 and went to a new post in Tokyo in November. As the workload was relatively light there, he made great progress in his writing of *Bibliographie Coréenne*. He requested reference materials from Bishop Mutel in Korea and studied Korean books in the collections of Japan's Imperial Library in Ueno and Zojoji Temple, during which he encountered the *Tripitaka Koreana*, taken to Japan in the 15th century. Volume 1 of *Bibliographie Coréenne* was published in 1894.

While in Tokyo, his first two sons, Charles and Louis were born. Once he had a family, Courant expressed difficulties with having to move around every few years. In 1895, despite his request to be sent to Seoul, he was transferred to the consulate in Tianjin. But while in China, tragedy befell his family: his two sons contracted cholera and later died on the same day. This terrible incident made him want to abandon interpretation and look for a new career. For this reason, he returned to Paris. In 1896, another son was born and named Charles after his firstborn.

Also in 1896, the third volume of *Bibliographie Coréenne* was published. Regrettably, this did not bring Courant the academic recognition he so deserved. Despite the amount of hours and effort he put into it and the value of the materials of which it consists, academic circles of the time were unaware of Korea and did not appreciate its worth nor make proper use of it. It won praise from only a handful of Orientalists, although it did win him an Academie award. Daniel Bouchez found the reason in the ambiguity inherent in *Bibliographie Coréenne*. Namely, a bibliography is not meant to be perused, but instead, treated as a specialty publication to be referred to, making it difficult for people to properly appreciate it. He believed that if the Introduction of 170 pages had been separately published, the situation would have been different. In fact, the Introduction alone has been published in translation several times.[4]

In 1897, Courant, who was looking for a new job in Paris, got an offer from the National Library of France to list up the Chinese publications in its collection. The job, at first thought to only require one or two years, was not completed even after 15 years as the library continued to buy new books. Even after he left the city in 1900, Courant came back to Paris to stay for two months every summer and carried on with the project, but when the last volume was published in 1912, it ended with Chapter 21 and the planned Chapters 22 and 23 were never published. Despite the

---

4) Daniel Bouchez, "Maurice Courant, the Pioneer of Korean Studies Part 1," trans. Jeon Su-yeon, *Journal of Korean Studies* 51 (1986): 174. The translation of the Introduction is dealt with in the latter part of this paper.

initially planned title, *Catalog of Chinese, Korean and Japanese Books* (*Catalogue des livres chinois, coréen et japonais*), the Chinese chapters were never completed. Still, this job allowed Courant to come across many books and increase his academic capabilities.

Despite difficult circumstances, Courant never stopped his studies of Korea. In February 1897, he gave a lecture at the Guimet Museum entitled, "Korean-Japanese Relations until the Ninth Century and Effects on the Origin of Japanese Culture" by comparing Korea's *Samguk Sagi* (*History of the Three Kingdoms*) and *Nihon Shoki* (*Chronicles of Japan*). The same year, he presented a paper entitled, "Korea's Pansori and Dance," and in 1898, "Stele of the Goguryeo Kingdom," the West's first research paper on the Gwanggaeto Stele found in 1875. In December 1899, he explained Korean rites that appealed to supernatural beings in a lecture entitled, "History and Overview of Korea's Religious Rites," given at the Guimet Museum again.

In early 1898, Collin de Plancy suggested to Courant that he write a report on Korea to present at the 1900 Paris Exposition. However, despite all that he achieved with regard to Koreanology, his Korean studies did not help him embark on a new career as he wanted. He had wanted a professorial position at L´Ecole des Langues Orientales since 1897, but by 1899, this had come to nothing, with either its Chinese or Japanese department. In December 1899, he received the opportunity to teach Chinese and on "daily life in China" at Lyon's Chamber of Commerce and Industry and the University of Lyon. Things were unstable for some time, but in 1903, the university established a degree course on Chinese studies. After that, Courant presented many academic findings on China, Japan, and Korea. In 1904 in particular, he presented papers on the situation Korea faced, surrounded by larger powers as it was, including "Korea and the Foreign Powers (La Corée et les puissances étrangères)" and "A Japanese Settlement in Korea – Busan since the 15th Century (Un établissement japonais en Corée, Pou-san depuis XVè siècle)."

In 1913, Courant received a doctoral degree from the University of Lyon with his paper, "Essay on the History of Chinese Classical Music, with an appendix on Korean Music (Essai historique sur la musique classique des Chinois, avec un qppendice relatif à la musique corèenne)" and was appointed a full professor at the university. He was 48 years old. However, three years prior, he had suffered a serious injury. While climbing a ladder outside a bookcase, he fell when it topped and his right arm crashed through a glass panel. With glass shards stuck deep in his wrist, he could no longer use his right hand. He learned how to use his left hand instead, but things were never the same after this life-changing accident. Also, the international situation surrounding Korea was becoming dire.

In 1919, Courant earned the opportunity to stay in Japan for six weeks as part of a university delegation for educational cooperation with that nation. During the trip, he visited Pyongyang, Seoul, and Daegu. While in Seoul, he reunited with Bishop Mutel and visited the Jangseogak Library.

Back in France, Courant's misfortune continued both at home and at work. He and his wife separated in 1921 due to her "prodigal habits," bringing an end to their marriage of 28 years and their two sons, Charles and Jean, 25 and 19 years of age at the time, had problems that required a guardian. Courant rented a small room in Lyon, where he lived out the rest of his days. From the separation until 1926, he participated actively in the university's administration and education, and during the last seven years of his time there - from 1927 until he had to retire due to an illness - he lectured on Korea. Examples of his lectures include "Korea from 1567 to 1644," "The Launch of a New Dynasty in 1392", and "Korean Kings and Politicians from the 14th to the 16th Centuries." They were believed to be very bold and yet difficult attempts in consideration of Korea's then diplomatic situation under Japan's oppressive colonial rule.

In 1933, he had to stop lecturing due to exhaustion and took a long holiday in a southern province. After that, he resumed teaching but had to stop everything after a stroke in early 1934. After a battle with the results of that stroke, Courant died on August 18, 1935 in Caluire. His first son Charles, unmarried, had died before him in 1930, while Jean, the second son, married in 1936 but died in 1950 without children.

Publications written and collected by Maurice Courant

Maurice Courant wrote a total of 103 books and papers throughout his life. Twenty-one[5] are about Korea, including *Bibliographie Coréenne*, which is regarded by Western academia as an essential part of the study of Korea to this day. They are as follows:

1) *Historical Repertoire of Korean Administration*
   "Répertoire histoique de l´administation corénne, 2 vol.," 1891.

2) "Historical Note on the Diverse Currencies used on the Korean Peninsula"
   "Note historique sur les diverses espéces de monnaie qui ont été usitées en Coree." *Journal asiatique*, 9~II(1983), pp. 270~289.

3) *Bibliographie Coréenne*
   "*Bibliographie coréenne", Tableau littéraire de la Corée*, Paris, Paris, E. Leroux, 1894-1896, 1901.

4) "Principal Periods of History on the Korean Peninsula"
   "Principales péiodes de histoire de la Corée," *Revue francaise du Japon*, 1985, pp. 1~9, 127~146 et 179~186, 1896, pp. 131~142 et 179~185.

---

5) Lee Hui-jae, "Essay on Maurice Courant and *Bibliographie Coréenne*," *Sookmyung Women's University Collection of Dissertations* 28 (1988): 330-335.

5) "Note on the Different Systems of Characters Employed in Korea"
"Note sur les different systèmes d´ériture employé en Coree,"
Transactions of the Asiatic Society of Japan, ⅩⅩⅧ, décembre 1895,
pp. 5~23.

6) "Traditional Korean Plays and Ballet"
"La complainte mime ét le ballet en Corée" *Journal asiatique,* 9~Ⅹ
(1897), pp. 74~76.

7) "Korean-Japanese Relations until the Ninth Century and the Effects
of the Korean Peninsula on the Origin of Japanese Civilization"
"La Coré jusqu´au Ⅸ°siecle, ses rapports avec le Japon et son influence
sur les origines de la civilisation japonaise," *T´oung pao* 通報, 1898,
pp. 1~7.

8) "Goguryeo Kingdom Stele in China"
"Stèle chinoise du royaume de Ko Kou Rye" *Journal asiatique,*
9~ⅩⅠ (1898), pp. 210~238.

9) "Note on the Studies of Korea and Japan"
"Note sur les études coréennes et japonaises," *Actes du onzieme congres
international des orientalistes, paris,* 1897, 2°section, Paris, Imprimerie
national, 1899, pp. 67~94.

10) "Summarized History of Korea's Religious Rites"

"Sommaire et historique des cultes coréns," conféence faite au Musé Guimet le 17 decémbre 1899, *T´oung pao* 通報, 1900, pp. 295~326.

11) *The Korean Pavilion at Champ de Mars, Memory of Seoul*
   "*Le pavillon corén au Champ de Mars, Souvenir de Seoul, Coree,*"Paris. Exposition universelle, 1900, pp. Ⅲ~Ⅷ.

12) "Several Korean Monuments"
   "Quelqus monuments coréens", *Conférence faite au Musée Guimet le 23* (1900) inédite (unpublished).

13) *Catalog of Chinese, Korean and Japanese Books*
   Bibliothèque nationale, Départment des manuscrits, *Catalogue des livres chinois, coréens et japonais,* 7 fascicules reliés en 2 volumes, Paris, 1900⊠1910; fascicule 8, Paris, 1912.

14) "Korea and the Foreign Powers"
   "La Coré et les puissances érangès," *Annales des sciences politiques,* Paris, 15 mars 1904, pp. 253~267.

15) *Situation of the Far East, Court of Korea*
   "Choses d´Extreme-Orient. La Cour de Corée."
   A reference for the *Journal des debats* dated April 6, 1904.

16) "A Japanese Settlement in Korea – Busan since the 15th Century"
   "Un éablissement japonais en Corée, pou-San depuis le ⅩⅤ° sièle,"

Annales coloniales, août-octobre 1904. Aussi en brochure dans Bibliothèque de la France coloniale moderne, Paris, 1904, p. 24.

17) "Korea"
"La Coré," dans Claudius MADROLLE, La Chine de Nord, paris, Comité de L´Asie française, 1904, VII-14-36-144-6p. Réé.: *La Nord-Est de la Chine,* Paris, Hachette, 1913.

18) "From Alliance to Domination – Steps of a Protectorate"
"De l´alliance à la domination. Etapes d´un protectorat," *Annales coloniales.*
Paris, 11 novembre 1909.

19) "Essay on the History of Chinese Classical Music, with an appendix on Korean Music" *Essai historique sur la musique classique des Chinois, avec un qppendice relatif à la musique corèenne,* fascicule séparé (n°8), Paris, Ch. Delagrave, 1912, p. 241.

20) Article "Korea," *Encyclopedia of Religion and Ethics,* edited by James HASTINGS, Aberdeen 1908~1915, rééd.: Edinburgh, 1925, 13 vol. 7 (1914), pp. 744~758.

21) "Korean Characters"
"Lécriture coréenne," *Notices sur les caractèes érangers, anciens et modernes,* Paris, Imprimerie nationale, 1927, pp. 307~309.

Photo 3: Collège de France library

In the Introduction of *Bibliographie Coréenne*, Courant wrote, "I searched every bookstore in Seoul and looked through every book they had. I bought books that seemed most interesting and made detailed notes about the others." He marked the books he bought as "M.C." in *Bibliographie Coréenne*, which totaled 366 volumes of 84 books.[6] Courant's

---

6) Publications from Maurice Courant's personal collection that are listed in *Bibliographie Coréenne* are as follows: 3. 千字文 12. 童蒙先習 29. 簡禮彙纂 67-II. 御定奎章全 68-II. 全韻玉篇 285bis 退陶先生自省錄 582bis 文節公遺稿 631-II. 四溟集 768. 剪燈新話 1047. 五禮儀 1053. 三班禮式 1068-I. 四禮便覽 1069. 四禮撮要 1073. 喪禮備要 1077. 五服名義 1156. 俎豆錄 1181. 忠烈祠志 1305. 進饌儀軌 1316. 喪禮補編 1461. 大典會通 1462. 六典條例 1467. 百惠要覽 1517. 銀臺便攷 1525. 兩銓便攷 1694. 通文館志 1723. 燕行事例 1726. 図禮摠覽 1744. 同文考略 1777. 大明律

private collection was sold to the IHEC (Institut des Hautes Études Chinoises) of the Collège de France over two occasions in 1936. As Courant died in August 1935 and the college first bought his books on January 15, 1936, it seems that his collection was sold only after his death.[7]

Composition and Content of *Bibliographie Coréenne*

Bibliographie Coréenne is a massive work consisting of an introduction, which amounts to 171 pages and can be a separate book in its own right, and lists of 3,821 items in different areas, complete with annotations. The

附例 1835. 三國史記 1850. 高麗史 1851-III. 東國通鑑 1857. 麗史提綱 1861. 東國通鑑提綱 1864. 紀年兒覽 1910. 璿源系譜紀略 1921. 東國文獻錄 2030. 赤鼠錄 2079. 篆韻便覽 2105-II. 攷事撮要 2108. 大東韻府群玉 2112. 東國文獻備考 2116. 後自警編 2187. 天下諸國圖 2195. 海左全圖 2196-II. 大東與地圖 2207. 漢陽全圖 2211. 東京全圖 2214. 湖南地圖 2215. 無題[全州] 2218. 龜城地圖 2223. 宜和奉使高麗圖經 2229. 朝鮮志 2236. 鷄林志 2279. 南漢伽藍誌 2292. 東京雜記 2316. 海東諸國記 2366. 天象列次分野之圖 2573. 梁琴新譜 2811. 大朝鮮大法國條約 3104. 近世朝鮮政鑑 3387. 上尊號文 3388. (無題)[敍壬帖] 3408. 揭付各廳 3419. 法規類編續 3491. 御製閱武亭四井記帖 3516. 經理朝鮮右僉都御史楊公去思碑 3519. 遲遲臺碑銘帖 3520. 御製花山龍珠寺奉佛祈福偈 3523. 大淸皇帝功德碑 3525. 大唐平百濟國碑銘 3530. 紛條制札 3532-III. 陜州東海碑 3540. 句麗古碑 3541. 御製釋王寺碑文 3573. 圓簡公神道碑銘 3577. 思彦君墓碑文 3585. 御製文孝世子神道碑銘帖 3586. 孝惠公神道碑謄本 3596. 御製李忠武公碑帖 3675. 新法地平日晷 3676. 簡平日晷 3736. 祕密敎.

7) Recorded on the register of the Collège de France are "1er acht Courant (Courant, 1st purchase)," '2e acht Courant (Courant, 2nd purchase)," and more. The second purchase is not dated and is indicated only with the no. of expenditure (Dép. n° 79-1935-1936). Professor Daniel Bouchez remarked in the preface to *Bibliographie Coréenne – Revised and Translated* that materials purchased by Maurice Courant were repurchased by the IHEC of the Collège de France. Lee Hye-eun and Lee Hui-jae, "Status of and Possible Ways to Use Old Korean Books in the Collection of the Collège de France," *Journal of the Korean Society for Library and Information Science* 45(4) (2011): 244.

Introduction was printed with Courant's preface in 1894 at the Tokyo Tsukiji Kappan Seizosho (Tokyo Tsukiji Type Foundry, 東京筑地活版制造所).[8]

Each of the Introduction's six untitled chapters describes what Korea was like when Courant wrote *Bibliographie Coréenne* and difficulties he had with writing. Then it goes on to talk about Korea's publications, characters, philosophies, literature, and more and introduce books related to the content in the body. It deals, in a systematic way, with the languages and characters that constitute the content of the books; their physical aspects; and their intellectual and artistic content covering philosophies, academic subjects, arts and culture. It even looks at book distribution from a modern perspective, which was unprecedented in Courant's day. Such descriptions of bookstores and book rental shops of the time cannot be found anywhere else.

A brief look into the content and composition of the Introduction[9] reveals that Chapter I describes Korean books and bookstores in the late 19th century. It also records the author's motive for and background to his writing of the bibliography and confesses difficulties associated with writing about Korean books. Such difficulties include the various forms

---

8) Indicated at the end of each of Volumes 1, 2, and 3 of *Bibliographie Coréenne* is "Printed by Tokyo Tsukiji Kappan Seizosho (Tokyo Tsukiji Type Foundry) Corp. at 17, Tsukiji 2nd Street, Kyobashi District, Tokyo, Japan (大日本東京市京橋區築地貳丁目十七番地 株式會社東京築地活版製造所印行)." As the supplement was published in 1901, it is believed to have been printed in France.
9) What follows is based on: Lee Hui-jae, *Bibliographie Coréenne – Revised and Translated* (original work by Maurice Courant) (Seoul: Ilchokak, 1994).

of Korean names: last names, first names, courtesy names, pen names, titles given by the king, posthumous titles, and public post names. It also looks at geographic names according to different dynasties and confusion deriving from use of the same geographic names as China's, use of the sexagenary cycle, years of a king's reign, Chinese era names, and more.

Chapter II is about Korean books. It illustrates the making and characteristics of traditional *hanji* (Korean paper), printing, and physical characteristics of old Korean books. Courant wrote, "Printing has long been used in Korea and reached a considerable level of skill, but with the very high prices for printed books, transcription has continued. Transcribed books come in various formats, ranging from folios to small octavos. Some are written in simplified characters while others are graciously written to look like printed books."

Chapter III covers characters used in Korean. It deals with the introduction of Chinese characters to the Korean peninsula and their use, invention of the Idu script, comparison of the languages of Korea, Japan, and China, and invention of the Hangeul alphabet.

Chapter IV concerns philosophies in Korea. It explains the introduction of Buddhism, Taoism, and Confucianism to Korea, and the role of the latter and its importance to gaining an understanding of Korean history. Courant commented that Confucianism in Korea created a high level of sternness in various aspects of life, which was not seen in China, and motivated the creation of different political factions. Chinese publications were continuously republished and discussed.

Chapter V deals with Korean publications written in Chinese characters about poetry, rites and administration, history, geography, the sciences, medicine, military tactics, foreign language education, and more. Here Courant broke down Korean literature and academic subjects in this manner, providing a basic foundation, and discussed them in relation to the publications listed in the book's main bibliography.

Finally, Chapter VI handles publications in Hangeul, including popular novels and story books enjoyed by the general public and Hangeul publications after the introduction of Catholicism and Protestantism.

As a quick overview of the body, which follows the Introduction and is comprised of lists and annotations, what follows below are the composition of each part and chapter, the listing no. of listed publications, and the number of such publications:

Part I   Education (Enseignement), vol. 1, pp. 1-38

Chapter 1.   Education, n°1-26 (26)

　　ch. 2.   Epistolary manuals (Manuels épostolaires), n°27-42 (16)

　　ch. 3.   Various manuals (Manuels divers), n°43-46 (4)

Part II   Studies of languages, vol. 1, pp. 39-115

Chapter 1.   Chinese language (Langue chinoise), n°47-95 (49)

　　ch. 2   Manchurian language (Langue mantchoue), n°96-119 (24)

　　ch. 3.   Mongolian language (Langue mongole), n°120-140 (21)

As the above quick view of the 3,821 books covered in 36 chapters in 9 parts reveals, although Courant mentioned the *Siku Quanshu Zongmu Tiyao* (*Annotated Catalog of the Complete Imperial Library,* 四庫全書總目) as an important reference catalog used in his writing of *Bibliographie Coréenne*, he did not adopt the traditional quartering method (*jing shi si ji*, 經史子集) of book classifications widely used in China and Korea, but used his own classification method instead. This captures the attention of academic circles in the history of taxonomy. The traits of his classifications are as follows:

Part I (education) includes educational books (e.g. Hangeul education, *Thousand Character Classic*, *Hunmongseo* for children's education); epistolary manuals (letters and various forms); and various manuals (petitions, reports, and homemaking).

The Chinese language accounts for the largest portion of Part 2 (studies of languages), which is divided into general books (e.g. rime dictionaries and character dictionaries) and teaching materials for Chinese-Korean and Korean-Chinese interpretation. Other chapters deal with Manchurian, Mongolian, Japanese, and Sanskrit.

From a Western perspective, the books under Part 3 (Confucianism), numbering only a few, could have been grouped together into a single chapter of classic philosophies (Philosophie Classique). Still, Courant divided them into three chapters of Confucian classics (eight items), works about Confucius, and classical philosophies by Confucian scholars, which fall under the traditional *si* classification. This indicates that Courant used both his own classifications and the East's traditional classifications of old books. The eight items in Chapter 1 are the *General Collection* (Collection generale), the *Book of Changes* (Livre des transformation), the *Book of Documents* (Livre des histoire), the *Book of Odes* (Livre des odes), the *Book of Rites* (Livre des rites), the *Spring and Autumn Annals* (*Printemps et automne*), the Four Books (Livres classiques), and the *Book of Filial Duty* (*Livre des piete filiale*), revealing a focus on the traditional classics.

Part 4 (literature) lists the second largest number of books after Part 5. Its chapters handle poetry, anthologies of prose, novels, and miscellaneous works (e.g. quotations, reflections, essays). Each chapter consists of Chinese literature as well as Chinese-language literature in Korea and Korean literature. These anthologies, novels, and miscellaneous works provide valuable insights into Korean literature.

Part 5 (manners and customs) lists the largest number of books at 777. It is divided into rites and administration: the former covers customs, ancestral ritual formalities, various court ceremonies, and national funerals. The latter consists of general administration; writings bestowed by the royal family and those presented by retainers to the king; the royal family, the Cabinet, etc.; the six ministers of personnel, taxation, rites, military affairs, punishments, and public works; relations with China; and more. The books in the sections on ancestral ritual formalities (n° 1110-1193), various court ceremonies (1194-1315), and national funerals (1316-1445) are mostly various *Uigwe* books in the collection of the National Library of France. They are mostly indicated with simple information such as their titles and collections. *Uigwe* refers to a vast collection of books recording in detail the royal rituals and ceremonies of the Joseon dynasty and had been kept in the Oegyujanggak library on Ganghwa Island, not far from Seoul. As Courant acknowledges, Admiral Roze brought them to France in 1886, where they had been retained in the National Library of France. Created by the court and central government offices, they are works of art in their own right, beautifully handwritten on quality paper and bound with silk. Koreans had endeavored for their return, which has been done in the form of permanent rental and currently in the care of the National Museum of Korea.

Part 6 (history and geography) has four chapters: The first chapter (Korean history) features histories of Korea, chronological tables, books of examples, royal genealogy books and biographies, general genealogy books and biographies, and special histories. The second chapter (documents related to Korea) includes various records on Korea including administration forms, old documents, bibliographies, archeology and paleography books, collections of penmanship, poetry and painting, and encyclopedias. The third chapter (Chinese history) also consists of histories of China, chronological tables, books of examples, biographies, and special histories. The fourth chapter (geography) includes maps, course records, descriptions and travelogs of Korea, and descriptions and travelogs of China and Japan.

Part 7 (sciences and arts) consists of eight chapters. Chapters 1, 4, 6, 7, and 8 are about mathematics, military art, agriculture and sericulture, music, and arts, without breaking down the topics into subcategories. Chapter 2 (astronomy & cosmography) divides into calendars, solar and lunar eclipse, astronomical charts, and celestial maps; Chapter 3 (divination) into astrology, theory of divination based on topography (地理經), interpretations of divination signs (卦辭), prophecies, etc.; and Chapter 5 (medicine) into medicine and veterinary science. They are further broken down due to their content, but there are relatively small numbers of books listed.

Under Part 8 (religion), Chapter 1 (Taoism) is comprised of Taoist scriptures; ritual formalities for the Demon-conquering Emperor (伏魔大帝), Saintly Emperor of the South Palace (南宮聖帝), and Fuyou (孚佑, Imperial Lord, Savior of the Needy); and various other books. Chapter 2 (Buddhism) consists of scriptures, precepts, treatises on the great patriarchs, sermons, prayers and Buddhist songs, and various other books. Chapter 3 (Catholicism) is broken down into general books, lives and histories of saints and the Christ, the Seven Sacraments, different aspects of the religion, prayers, and church histories in Korea and Japan.

Part 9 (external relations) consists of Chapter 1 (treaties and conventions), Chapter 2 (trade documents), and Chapter 3 (newspapers), together covering diplomatic relations, trade relations and newspapers.

In the meantime, the supplement to volumes I to III is composed the same as the supplement of 1901. They are mostly simple lists. What's important about the 1901 supplement is that it includes *Baegun Hwasang Chorok Buljo Jikji Simche Yojeol* as n° 3788. As this has been mentioned several times in the studies on *Jikji*, here in this article it is simply confirmed.

Recognition of *Bibliographie Coréenne*[10]

After publication of the first volume of *Bibliographie Coréenne* in 1894, Émmanuel-Édouard Chavannes (1865-1918), a sinologist who studied together with Courant at L´Ecole des Langues Orientales, introduced it in an academic journal issued by the Société Asiatique, as adding a new chapter of Korea to the history of Far Eastern civilization and its bibliography part as a result of painstaking research and perseverance over many years.[11] Not long after publication of the third volume in 1896, *Bibliographie Coréenne* became known to Korea. It was in "Bibliographie coreenne," an article contributed by Annie Holmes Kenmure (1857-1937), wife of a missionary named Alexander Kenmure (1856-1910), to *The Korean Repository* in 1897,[12] where the bibliography first appeared in any publication issued in Korea. The *Description of Korea (Описаніе Кореи)*, issued by the Russian Ministry of Finance in 1900, took much from the Introduction of *Bibliographie Coréenne* and restructured it.[13] In Chapter

---

10) Lee Hye-eun, "A Historical Approach to the Recognition and Research of Maurice Courant and *Bibliographie Coréenne*," *Cogito* 86 (2018): 39-68.
11) Édouard Chavannes, *Journal Asiatique* 9 (5) (Paris: Société asiatique, 1895), 539-542.
12) A. H. Kenmure, "Bibliographie coreene," *The Korean Repository* (Seoul: The Trilingual Press, 1897): 201-206 (June), 258-266 (July). This English translation wrote the French *Bibliographie Coréenne as* Bibliographie coreene and this is why no acute accent is used in the title.
13) Russian Ministry of Finance, *Description of Korea (Описаніе Кореи)*, trans. The Academy of Korean Studies (Seongnam: Jeongwang, 1984) (Составлено въ канцеляріи Министра Финансовъ, *Описаніе Кореи (съ картой)*, С.-Петербургъ : изданіе Министерства Финансовъ, типографія Ю. Н. Эрлиха 'Ju. N., 1900).

9 on Korean language, literature, and education in particular, "2. Letters (Chinese characters, Idu script, and Hangeul alphabet)" and "3. Literature" are practically translations of the Introduction of *Bibliographie Coréenne*.

In 1901, *The Korean Review* carried English translations by James Scarth Gale (1863-1937) of the parts on introducing Chinese characters into Korea[14] and the Idu script[15] from the Introduction of *Bibliographie Coréenne*. Kanazawa Shozaburo (金澤庄三郎, 1872-1967), a Japanese linguist, published in 1911 *Chosen Shoseki Mokuroku* (*Catalog of Korean Publications,* 朝鮮書籍目錄), a selection of 100 books from his own collection, and in its short foreword, cited Courant's *Bibliographie Coréenne* as four volumes of annotated lists of a whopping 3,800 books and the most complete inventory of Korean books.[16] The overview of *Chosen Kosho Mokuroku* (*Catalog of Old Korean Books,* 朝鮮古書目錄),[17] written by Asami Rintaro (淺見倫太郎, 1869-1943) who served as judge in Seoul from 1906 to 1918 and collected old Korean books, is a summary of Courant's Introduction.

In 1936, the academic journal of the Korea branch of the Royal Asiatic Society carried an English translation by W. Massy Royds of the

---

14) J. S. Gale, "The Introduction of Chinese into Korea, Translated from the Introduction to Courant's *Bibliographie Coreenne*," *The Korea Review* April (Seoul: The Methodist House, 1901): 155-163.
15) J. S. Gale, "The ni-t'u," *The Korea Review* July (Seoul: The Methodist House, 1901): 289-293.
16) Kanazawa Shozaburo (金澤庄三郎), *Chosen Shoseki Mokuroku (Catalog of Korean Publications,* 朝鮮書籍目錄) (Place of publication unknown: Kanazawa Shozaburo, 1911).
17) Chosen Kosho Kankokai (朝鮮古書刊行會), *Chosen Kosho Mokuroku (Catalog of Old Korean Books,* 朝鮮古書目錄) (Seoul: Chosen Kosho Kankokai, 1911).

Introduction to Courant's *Bibliographie Coreenne*.[18] In the foreword to the journal, Horace H. Underwood praised *Bibliographie Coréenne* as the most comprehensive and detailed work by a Westerner about Korean life and culture and explained that, though it had been introduced through *The Korean Repository* in 1897, few people in the English-speaking world knew of it despite its immense value as reference material. In consideration of this, the Society decided to translate and carry its Introduction again.[19]

In 1938, Ogura Chikao (小倉親雄, 1913-1991), who worked part-time at the Japanese Government-General of Korea library, translated Royds' English translation into Japanese and published in *Dokusho* (讀書) under the title of "Introduction to Maurice Courant's *Bibliographie Coréenne* (モリス・クラン 朝鮮書誌序論)."[20] Ogura Shinpei (小倉進平, 1882-1944), a Japanese linguist and professor at Keijo Imperial University and Tokyo Imperial University, briefly introduced in *Chosen Gogakushi* (*History of Korean Linguistics*, 朝鮮語學史) Maurice Courant and the background to his writing of *Bibliographie Coréenne* and critiqued it as the "most excellent annotated catalog of books attempted by a Westerner."[21]

---

18) W. Massy Royds, "Introduction to Courant's *Bibliographie Coreenne,*" *Transactions of the Korea branch of the Royal Asiatic Society* 25 (Seoul: Korea branch of the Royal Asiatic Society, 1936): 1-100.

19) Horace H. Underwood, "Foreword," *Transactions of the Korea branch of the Royal Asiatic Society* (Seoul: Korea branch of the Royal Asiatic Society, 1936).

20) Ogura Chikao (小倉親雄), "Introduction to Maurice Courant's *Bibliographie Coréenne* (モリス⊠クラン 朝鮮書誌序論)," *Dokusho* (讀書) 2 (3) (Seoul: Chosen Dokusho Renmei (朝鮮讀書聯盟), 1938): 1-31.

21) Ogura Shinpei (小倉進平), *Zotei Chosen Gogakushi* (增訂 朝鮮語學史) (Tokyo: Toko Shoin, 1940), 53-55.

In a nutshell, Courant's *Bibliographie Coréenne* was introduced through English translations of its Introduction and then it was translated into Japanese. These writings and translations helped change the misunderstanding of Westerners who thought Korea did not produce any of its own books[22] and made them finally aware of Korea's books and long literary culture.

In 1946, Kim Su-gyeong (1918-2000), a Korean linguist, published in a separate book a Korean translation of the Introduction to *Bibliographie Coréenne* under the title of *Introduction to the History of Joseon Culture.*[23] As Kim affirmed, this was the first-ever translation into Korean of the Introduction and further significant in that it was finally translated by a

Photo 4: Translated versions by Kim Su-gyeong (1946, 1947)

22) Lee, *Bibliographie Coréenne - Revised and Translated*, 1.
23) Kim Su-gyeong, *Introduction to the History of Joseon Culture* (original work by Maurice Courant) (Seoul: Beomjonggak, 1946).

Korean 50 years after the publication of *Bibliographie Coréenne*.[24]

Following Kim's translation, several Korean translations have been published, but all were only of the Introduction. The publication of *Bibliographie Coréenne - Revised and Translated* (韓國書誌-修訂飜譯版)[25] in 1994 provided an opportunity for studies on Maurice Courant to expand. The reason the 1994 version came with "*Revised and Translated*" as its subtitle was that the translator did not stop at just translating, but conducted research to confirm the locations of the books listed, went over the original text for comparison, and indicated errors found in footnotes. Unlike the previous translations limited only to the Introduction, this version is the first Korean translation that includes the bibliography of all 3,821 books.

In July 2005, this revised and translated version was republished in CD-ROM and database formats to allow for easy search by researchers and increase its usage. Lee Hui-jae, the translator, expressed in the revised and translated version her hopes for further studies by herself and other researchers to identify any parts that may be major issues in *Bibliographie Coréenne*.[26] She found significance in that the revised and translated version was published in the 100th year of initial publication of *Bibliographie Coréenne in* 1894.

In the latter half of the 1960s, Korean society began taking interest in

---

24) Ibid., 190-191. Kim stated so based on 1896, the publication year of Vol. 3.
25) Lee, *Bibliographie Coréenne - Revised and Translated.*
26) Lee, Ibid., vii.

Korean materials in the possession of France. Against this background, new light was shed on achievements by Maurice Courant, on whom the Korean government posthumously conferred the Order of Cultural Merit on March 27, 1970 for his great contribution to introducing Korean culture overseas.[27] His meritorious service was defined as "laying the very basic groundwork for the development of Korean culture and introducing the true aspects of Korea overseas."[28]

Photo 5:
"Order of Cultural Merit Conferred to Maurice Courant" (*Dong-A Ilbo*, March 30, 1970)

Photo 6:
Bibliographie Coréenne - Revised and Translated (Book from 1994, CD-ROM from 2005)

27) "Order of Cultural Merit Conferred to the Late Maurice Courant, French Author of *Bibliographie Coréenne*," *Maeil Business Newspaper*, Mar. 28, 1970.
28) *The Dong-A Ilbo*, Mar. 30, 1970.

Conclusion: Maurice Courant and significance of *Bibliographie Coréenne*

The first, second, and third volumes of *Bibliographie Coréenne* were published in 1894, 1895, and 1896, respectively, and continuously revised until a supplement was published in 1901. Written in the late 19th and early 20th centuries before the term Koreanology even existed, *Bibliographie Coréenne* is a vast bibliography of old Korean books and provides important clues to their situation at the end of the Joseon dynasty. For its value as a reference, it is regarded as indispensible by many researchers of Koreanology to this day.

The ties between Maurice Courant and Korea began when he arrived in Seoul as a secretary interpreter on May 23, 1890 and have continued to today, not only through *Bibliographie Coréenne* but also a number of research papers related to Korea.

Courant's *Bibliographie Coréenne* was initially translated and introduced by Westerners and then quoted and referred to by Japanese in their writings before coming to have an impact on studies by Koreans. As such, it can be said that the academic network for understanding not only Korea's history and culture but also its books and literary culture at the end of the Joseon dynasty originated from Maurice Courant.

Studies on Maurice Courant by Koreans began when Kim Su-gyeong translated its Introduction into Korean in 1946, 50 years after the publication of the third volume of *Bibliographie Coréenne*. The full version, including the lists of books, was translated in 1994, 100 years after publication of the first volume. It was after this that *Bibliographie Coréenne* came to fully function as a bibliography in Korea, and in response, Korean academic circles have since produced excellent outcomes from research on *Bibliographie Coréenne* as if to make up for the lost centennial.

Besides the value *Bibliographie Coréenne* has in terms of the science of bibliography, the interest, affection, and effort shown by Maurice Courant toward Korea were never lost amid the historic upheavals of the fall of the Korean Empire and the severance of diplomatic relations between Korea and France, and laid the most important groundwork for the development of Koreanology today.

Bibliography

Asami, Rintaro (淺見倫太郎). *Chosen Geibunshi* (朝鮮藝文志). Seoul: Japanese Government-General of Korea, 1912.

Bodet, Frédéric. *Roman d'un voyageur: Victor Collin de Plancy, l'histoire des collections coréennes en France* (Paris: Cité de la céramique Sèvres et Limoges, 2015).

Bouchez, Daniel. "Maurice Courant, the Pioneer of Korean Studies Part 1." *Journal of Korean Studies* 51, translated by Jeon Su-yeon (Seoul: Institute of Korean Studies of Yonsei University, 1986): 153-194.

Bouchez, Daniel. "Maurice Courant, the Pioneer of Korean Studies Part 2." *Journal of Korean Studies* 52, translated by Jeon Su-yeon (Seoul: Institute of Korean Studies of Yonsei University, 1986): 83-121.

Courant, Maurice. "Korean Books and Culture." *Humanities Review* (人文評論) 3 (2), translated by Kim Su-gyeong (Seoul: Inmunsa, 1941): 14-25.

Chavannes, Édouard. *Journal asiatique* 9(5) (Paris: Société asiatique, 1895): 539-542.

Chosen Kosho Kankokai (朝鮮古書刊行會). *Chosen Kosho Mokuroku* (*Catalog of Old Korean Books,* 朝鮮古書目錄). Seoul: Chosen Kosho Kankokai, 1911.

Courant, Maurice. *Bibliographie Coréenne* (Paris: E. Leroux, 1894-1896, 1901).

Courant, Maurice. "Introduction to Maurice Courant's *Bibliographie Coréenne*

(モリス・クラン朝鮮書誌序論)," translated by Ogura Chikao (小倉親雄). Seoul: Ogura Chikao, 1941.

French School of the Far East and Korea University Museum. *Memory of Seoul: Korea and France, 1886-1905*. Seoul: Korea University Museum, 2006.

Gale, J. S. "The Introduction of Chinese into Korea, Translated from the introduction to Courant's *Bibliographie Coreenne*." *The Korea Review* April (Seoul: The Methodist House, 1901): 155-163.

Gale, J. S. "The ni-t'u." *The Korea Review* July (Seoul: The Methodist House, 1901): 289-293.

Han, Ji-hui, Kim, Hyo-gyeong, and Lee, Hye-eun. "Study of Rare Korean Books in the Collection of the National Library of France's Department of Manuscripts." *Bibliography Research* 69 (Seoul: Institute of Korean Bibliography, 2017): 307-325.

Hotel Drouot. *Collection d'un amateur: Objets d'art de la corée, de la Chine et du Japon, 27-30 mars 1911* (Paris: Hotel Drouot, 1911).

Hwang, Jeong-ha. "Publication of *Jikji* and Account of Its Transmission to This Day." *History and Silhak* 35 (2008): 37-88.

Itagaki, Ryuuta (板垣竜太). "Kim Su-gyeong's Korean Language Study and Japan." *Revaluation of Kim Su-gyeong, a Linguist and Defector to North Korea*. (Kyoto: Doshisha Korea Research Center, 2015): 61-98.

Lee, Eun-ryeong and Lee, Sang-hyeon. "Letters from Maurice Courant and Three Portraits of the Scholar of Korean Studies: A Study on the Soul of a Young Scholar of Korean Studies Engraved in the PA-AP

File of Collin de Plancy."

Lee, Hui-jae. "Essay on Maurice Courant and *Bibliographie Coréenne*." *Sookmyung Women's University Collection of Dissertations* 28 (Seoul: Sookmyung Women's University Dissertation Editorial Committee, 1988): 325-364.

Lee, Hui-jae. "State of Old Korean Books Located in France and Development Directions." *Results of and Tasks for Collections of Old Korean Writings Overseas* (Seoul: National Library of Korea, 2011): 27-46.

Lee, Hye-eun and Lee, Hui-jae. "Status of and Possible Ways to Use Old Korean Books in the Collection of the Collège de France." *Journal of the Korean Society for Library and Information Science* 45 (4) (Seoul: Korean Society for Library and Information Science, 2011): 235-251.

Lee, Hye-eun and Lee, Eun-ryeong. *Preliminary Research on the Collin de Plancy Collection: With a Focus on Materials in France's Médiathèque du Grand Troyes*. Seoul: Overseas Korean Cultural Heritage Foundation, 2016.

Lee, Hye-eun. "Another *Bibliographie Coréenne*: Oreste Toutzevitch Note." *Cogito* 82 (Busan: Pusan National University Institute of Humanities Research, 2017): 450-477.

Lee, Hye-eun. "A Historical Approach to the Recognition and Research of Maurice Courant and *Bibliographie Coréenne*." *Cogito* 86 (2018): 39-68.

Lee, Jin-myeong. "State and Research Trends of Koreanology Materials in the Collections of the National Library of France and the National Institute for Oriental Languages and Civilizations." *Korean Studies* 2 (2003): 183-221.

Lee, Sang-hyeon. "Discovery of Korean Classic Writers and Pedigree of Western Bibliography." *The Journal of Humanities and Social Science 21* 8(4) (Seoul: Asia Culture Academy, 2017): 887-906.

Lee, Sang-hyeon and Lee, Eun-ryeong. "Change in the Distribution of Novels in the Late 19th Century and Old Novels as 'Ethnographies' – The Meaning in Modern Academic History of the Description of Old Korean Novels in Maurice Courant's *Bibliographie Coréenne*." *Comparative Literature* 59 (2013): 37-74.

Journaux officiels. *Journal officiel de la République française. Lois et décrets* 255 (Paris: Journaux officiels, 1943).

Kanazawa, Shozaburo (金澤庄三郎). *Chosen Shoseki Mokuroku (Catalog of Korean Publications, 朝鮮書籍目錄)*. Place of publication unknown: Kanazawa Shozaburo, 1911.

Kenmure, A. H. "Bibliographie coreene." *The Korean Repository* (Seoul: The Trilingual Press, 1897): 201-206 (June), 258-266 (July).

Kim, Chae-hyeon, Park, Sang-hyeon, and Lee, Sang-hyeon. *A Collection of Korean Classics by Japanese: Imperial Japan and Korean Classics*. Seoul: Bakmunsa, 2017.

Kim, Su-gyeong. *Introduction to the History of Joseon Culture* (original work by Maurice Courant). Seoul: Beomjonggak, 1946.

Kim, Hye-yeong and Kim, Tae-seoung. "My Father, Kim Su-gyeong." *Revaluation of Kim Su-gyeong, a Linguist and Defector to North Korea* (Kyoto: Doshisha Korea Research Center (同志社コリア研究センタ), 2015): 5-29.

Korea Research Institute for Library and Information, National Library of Korea. *Old Korean Books in the Collection of the Collège de France.* Seoul: National Library of Korea, 2012.

Royds, W. Massy. "Introduction to Courant's *Bibliographie Coreenne.*" *Transactions of the Korea branch of the Royal Asiatic Society 25* (Seoul: Korea branch of the Royal Asiatic Society, 1936): 1-100.

Ogura, Chikao. "Joseon seoji seoron (Introduction à la bibliographie de Joseon)." *Dokseo (Lecture)* livre 2 volume n°3 (Séoul: Fédération pour la lecture de Joseon, 1938).

Ogura, Chikao (小倉親雄). "Introduction to Maurice Courant's *Bibliographie Coréenne* (モリス・クラン朝鮮書誌序論)." *Dokusho* (Lecture, 讀書) 2 (3) (Seoul: Chosen Dokusho Renmei (朝鮮讀書聯盟), 1938): 1-31.

Ogura, Chikao. "Introduction to Maurice Courant's *Bibliographie Coréenne.*" *Chosen (朝鮮)* (Seoul: Japanese Government-General of Korea, 1940-1941): 304-315.

Ogura, Shinpei (小倉進平). *Zotei Chosen Gogakushi* (増訂 朝鮮語學史). Tokyo: Toko Shoin, 1940.

Pusan National University Institute of Humanities Research, Jeom Pil-jae Institute, and Collège de France Institute of Korean Studies Library, eds. *Soul of a Young Scholar of Korean Studies Engraved in the Collin de Plancy File*. Seoul: Somyung Books, 2017.

Underwood, Horace H. "Foreword." *Transactions of the Korea branch of the Royal Asiatic Society* (Seoul: Korea branch of the Royal Asiatic Society, 1936).

Yeolsang Journal of Classical Studies 44 (Seoul: Yeolsang Classic Research Society, 2015): 75-141.

Park Byeng-sen and
Jikji Simche Yojeol
(直指心體要節 *Anthology of*
Great Buddhist Priests' Zen Teachings)

Choi Junsik
Ewha Womans University

I

Who is Park Byeng-sen?

1. What makes her achievement so important?

Those interested in Korean culture to some degree have probably heard of Dr. Park Byeng-sen and her achievements. However, their knowledge is likely to be superficial, limited to the fact that she was the one who rediscovered a book printed with movable metal type. Apart from this fact, people are not well aware of what subject matter the book concerned itself with, why the discovery was so crucial, or why Park's achievement was such a great feat for the nation of Korea. Moreover, they have almost no knowledge of what she had to undergo to discover the book and to prove that it was printed with movable metal type.

As we know, the book Park discovered and conducted historical research on is the *Jikji simche yojeol, or Anthology of Great Buddhist Priests' Zen Teachings* (hereinafter "Jikji"), the world's oldest extant book printed with movable metal type. In fact, it is easy to assume that the rediscovery was an undemanding process. However, the actual process of rediscovering the book, now considered a part of UNESCO World Heritage, and proving that it is the oldest surviving product of movable metal type printing could not have been more difficult. Yet, most resources on this topic describe the process as if the book had been discovered by the National Library of France and were easily acknowledged as the oldest extant book printed with movable metal type. However, a closer examination of the rediscovery, a global sensation at the time, reveals that it resulted from a series of much more dramatic events than commonly expected. First and foremost, without Dr. Park Byeng-sen, this historic feat would not have been possible. Without her relentless passion and dedicated efforts, Korea and the rest of the world would not have come across this epitome of human progress, *Jikji*.

As well known, *Jikji* was purchased by Victor Collin de Plancy, the first French consul (chargé d'affaires) to Korea, between the late 19th and early 20th century, and, after a series of events, came to be housed at the National Library of France. However, no one had a clue about the book's whereabouts until Park's rediscovery. Presumably, people knew about the existence of such a book but did not know where exactly it was, akin to a pauper who fails to realize that there is a gold nugget right in his home safe. With a gold nugget in his possession, he is actually a rich man, but without the knowledge, he cannot but continue to live in poverty. That was exactly the situation that the

National Library of France found itself in as the institution continued to serve as a storage facility for the global treasure without even realizing it. In fact, being in possession of a book such as *Jikji* would constitute a great honor for any cultural organization because it is the only extant book of its kind in the world.

In these circumstances, it was Dr. Park Byeng-sen who resolved this problematic situation. She not only discovered *Jikji,* which had been long hidden in the library, but proved to the world, through untiring efforts, that it was printed with movable metal type. (As for the painstaking process of her rediscovery, it will be discussed later in this paper.) No amount of praise will do justice to what she has done for the world. As it happens, the fact that *Jikji* is the oldest book printed with movable metal type and that it was published in Korea in 1377 is written in full view on the book's front cover. It is said that *Jikji* originally consisted of two volumes; however, only the second volume has survived to the present day. Even the original front cover of the second volume had been torn away, with a new piece of paper attached in its place. That is probably why, on the cover of *Jikji,* Collin de Plancy (or Maurice Courant)[1] freely jotted down the book's

---

1) Collin de Plancy asked his subordinate Maurice Courant to write a bibliography of the books he collected in Korea. As a result, *Korean Bibliography* was published in three volumes during the years 1894–1896. It does not mention *Jikji,* but its supplement, published in 1902, does contain bibliographical information on *Jikji,* indicating that the book was purchased between 1896 and 1902. The supplement states that *Jikji* was

bibliographical information, which he had probably been informed of at the time of his purchase of the book.

In light of such circumstances, if the French librarians had paid more attention, they would have realized the precious value of the book. However, if I dare to hazard a guess, it appears that they did not regard what was written on its cover as a statement of fact. The idea that Gutenberg's 42-line bible is the oldest book printed with movable metal type was so deeply entrenched in their minds that they would not have been able to even consider another explanation. Most likely, they could not imagine that such a landmark invention in the history of the world actually took place in Asia, especially in Korea, deemed "uncivilized" and the least known Asian country, instead of in the "civilized" land of Europe. Perhaps, for this reason, they must have ignored the bibliographical information written on the cover of *Jikji*. If the cover page had said that it was the oldest book published in Europe with movable metal type, the librarians would not have ignored the book so easily. Ultimately, for Europeans, losing the

---

printed with movable metal type at Heungdeoksa Temple in Cheongju in 1377 and that the movable metal type was invented 26 years earlier than Gyemija, a movable metal type commissioned by King Taejong of Joseon.

Although there is a theory that the supplement was published in 1901, Park's book states that it was published in 1902, which was the year used above.

Park, B, (2002). *Han-kuk-ŭi in-swae* [Korean printing] (p. 86). Cheongju, Korea: Cheongju Early Printing Museum Press.

honor of being the inventor of movable metal type to a small East Asian country such as Korea would have put a dent in their pride. I will further discuss this point later in the study, but for now, I will say that it is not difficult to imagine how the Europeans surrounding Park would have reacted when she announced that *Jikji* was printed in Korea and was in fact the oldest surviving book printed with movable metal type.

Park had to cope with a great deal of European prejudice. That is, she had to struggle against their suspicion that Korea could not have produced such a book. Thus, she had to scientifically prove, by every possible means, that *Jikji* was made from movable metal type. At the time, there certainly must have been several experts well versed in bibliography, but no one paid attention to the book. I believe the reason behind this deliberate lack of attention was, as previously mentioned, a matter of European pride. On the other hand, as an expatriate from Korea, the country of *Jikji*'s origin, Park's position was completely different from that of the Europeans. There is a saying that goes, "All expatriates are patriots," so, in all likelihood, she must have wanted to prove that *Jikji*, the brainchild of Korea, was the world's oldest surviving book printed with movable metal type.

However, Park knew nothing about printing culture before she came across the book, which is understandable as she was a scholar of

Park introducing the photographed copy of *Jikji* to Korean scholars (Source: *Chosun Ilbo*, December 23, 1972)

Korean history and folk culture who had probably never thought about topics such as movable metal type and printing. Still, she immersed herself in learning about printing culture, a brand new subject, which is a testament to her greatness. Her new academic journey was a grand adventure, bordering on a doomed pursuit. In fact, it was a precarious effort to teach herself about subjects outside her own field later in life and meet with world-renowned scholars for discussion. Since other scholars of printing culture were already well aware of existing research findings, it must have been extremely challenging to stand alone against their preconceived ideas. Yet, she ventured into this virtually impossible task and eventually achieved her stated goal of proving that *Jikji* is the world's oldest extant book printed with movable metal type.

Park's success served as a source of much renown to two parties. Above all, the National Library of France was greatly honored by her discovery, which is more than understandable as the institution had unknowingly housed this singular book of world heritage. A book like *Jikji* is an honor to the institution or country that possesses it, not to the country of its origin. For instance, the Metropolitan Museum of Art in New York, U.S.A. is considered a great museum due to its collection of artifacts from diverse countries around the world, without regard to where the artifacts came from. In fact, France was able to possess this precious gem of a book thanks to the high level of cultural awareness of the French people. The fact that the National Library of France has such a book as *Jikji* is a testament to France's highly sophisticated humanities-based culture. It was the cultural understanding of the French people that enabled a man like Collin de Plancy, a diplomat and not a student of humanities, to recognize the value of *Jikji* and add it to his collection. However, the role of France in the rediscovery is limited to this, and it is Dr. Park Byeng-sen who deserves the full credit for giving the National Library of France the great honor of possessing the world's oldest surviving book printed with movable metal type.

The other party Park's discovery distinguished is, without a doubt, the Korean people. Thanks to *Jikji,* the Korean people were able to confidently announce to the world that Korea was the originator of movable metal type. Even before the rediscovery of *Jikji,* the Korean people had argued at home that Korea was the first country to use movable metal type; however, this argument had not been accepted internationally because it was based solely on historical records, not on physical evidence. As is well known, historical record has it that the *Sangjeong yemun* (詳定禮文 *Detailed and Authentic Code of Ritual*) was printed with movable metal type in 1234[2]. However, as the book has not survived to the present day, the claim had remained ignored by international academia.

It was against this backdrop that Park discovered *Jikji* and proved, through painstaking efforts, that it was the oldest book printed with movable metal type. Thanks to her endeavor, the Korean people were able to make stronger claims that Korea was the originator of metal type. Admittedly, even though *Jikji* is the oldest extant book printed with movable metal type, it is theoretically possible that Korea may not be the inventor of movable metal type. Perhaps, another country

---

2) This book was published some 200 years prior to the publication of Gutenberg's 42-line bible.

invented it, but all the books printed subsequently were lost. However, so far, no such book has been discovered. As such, thanks to Park, Korea is now acknowledged as the publisher of the world's earliest metal type printed book, with a high likelihood of being the inventor of the world's first movable metal type.

It is evident that most Korean people do not realize the significance associated with the invention of movable metal type in the cultural history of humanity. Using movable metal type, humanity came to print books in large numbers, which, in turn, dramatically improved the circulation and accumulation of knowledge. This was particularly true for the Western world, where Gutenberg's invention of movable type printing led to dramatic social changes, including religious, industrial, and scientific revolutions. Movable metal type printing was certainly the single greatest influence behind all these revolutions. For this reason, Gutenberg's invention is considered by some to be one of the most important moments in history over the past millenium.[3]

But isn't Korea the country that invented movable metal type and first printed books with the technology? As such, Korea came to be

---

3) For instance, *The Life Millennium*, published by *Time*, a renowned U.S.-based magazine, listed the invention of movable metal type among the 100 most important events of the past 1,000 years.

regarded as a country with a magnificent cultural history, with the honor of being the progenitor of movable metal type. Such global recognition was only made possible by Park's rediscovery of this unique treasure *Jikji* and her success in proving that it was a book printed with movable metal type. Thanks to her discovery and research, this ancient book became an artifact treasured by not only Korea and France but the entire global community. For this reason, in 2001, *Jikji* was inscribed on UNESCO's Memory of the World Register. There is an interesting backstory herein, which testifies as to how invaluable the book really is.

I heard this story directly from a member of the Korean National Commission for UNESCO. After submitting the application for the inscription, Korean authorities were deeply concerned because *Jikji* might fail to be inscribed on the Memory of the World Register because it was currently located not in Korea, the country of its origin, but in another country. Upon hearing about such concerns, UNESCO officials in charge of the inscription said that it does not matter where the book is being kept today and noted that the only thing that matters is the fact that *Jikji* is the world's oldest book printed with movable metal type. For this reason, the book was inscribed on the Register without any difficulties.

2. Park Byeng-Sen, Korea's Cultural Hero

I have always praised Dr. Park Byeng-sen as one of Korea's cultural heroes because what she has done is larger than life, a feat that cannot be achieved by an ordinary person. Although not very well known, she endured a great deal of criticism and jealousy for verifying that *Jikji* is the oldest extant book printed with movable metal type. To make matters worse, she was fired from the library, years after the verification, when she also discovered *Uigwe*, or the Royal Protocols of the Joseon Dynasty. Those who are unfamiliar with her stories behind the scenes may think that she discovered *Jikji* fairly easily and that its status as the world's oldest movable metal type printed book was recognized when, in 1972, the National Library of France held an exhibition of ancient books to celebrate the "International Book Year."

However, the road to such international acclaim was not smooth at all. Park did not receive any support from Korea, her homeland, nor from her library, which did nothing but cast a suspicious eye. Despite such obstacles, she did not waver; instead, she taught herself about metal type printing and proved, after a prolonged period of experiments and research, that *Jikji* was a book printed with movable metal type. This is why I consider her a hero. In spite of the jealousy and ostracism toward her, she pushed toward her goal and achieved success, which itself is worthy of great respect. Yet, her endeavor was not for her own personal gains, but to promote the cultural advancement of her homeland and humanity, which makes her a true hero.

Truth be told, there are quite a few Korean cultural heroes when it comes to UNESCO's Memory of the World. There are other items of Korean documentary heritage inscribed on the Memory of the World Register, including the Haerye Edition *of Hunminjeongeum*, the *Annals of the Joseon Dynasty* and the Printing Woodblocks of the *Tripitaka Koreana*. The stories behind the preservation and survival of these books are as dramatic as the story behind *Jikji*. As for the Haerye Edition of *Hunminjeongeum*, the famous private collector Jeon Hyeong-pil (1906–1962) bought it at a price equivalent to the value of ten tile-roofed (meaning "luxurious") houses and kept it. It is said that during the Korean War (1950–1953), he always carried it with him on his person. Similarly, the *Annals of the Joseon Dynasty* faced the risk of being burned to ashes by the Japanese forces that invaded Joseon during the Japanese invasions of Korea (1592–1598). For protection, An Ui and Son Heung-rok relocated the Annals from the Jeonju History Archive to a shelter in Naejangsan Mountain and kept it there for a year before returning the treasure to the government of Joseon. Likewise, the Printing Woodblocks of the *Tripitaka Koreana* was able to survive the Korean War, thanks to

Colonel Kim Yeong-hwan of the ROK Air Force who refused to follow the order to bomb Haeinsa Temple. All these documentary treasures are vulnerable to fire damage as they are made of paper or wood. Without the venerable acts of the aforementioned cultural heroes, none of them would have survived.

The same holds true for *Jikji*. Without Park, its whereabouts or existence would have been completely unknown. In this regard, Dr. Park Byeng-sen, who rediscovered the book and proved its outstanding universal value, is a true hero.

II

Park's Path to the Discovery of *Jikji*

So far, we have examined what Park has done and how significant her achievement is. Now, before delving deeper into her work, let's look briefly at what *Jikji* really is because prior knowledge about the book will help us better understand her efforts. To begin with, the significance of *Jikji* does not lie in its content, but in the fact that it is a book printed with movable metal type and in how she came to discover the book. Thus, I will focus on what she did, after briefly explaining the content of the book.

1. What is *Jikji*?

The original title of *Jikji* is lengthy: *Baegun hwasang chorok buljo jikji simche yojeol*. As previously mentioned, instead of the verbose title, the front cover of the book is adorned merely with "jikji," presumably the most crucial word in the original title. The author (or possibly compiler) of the book is Baegun Hwasang, the first part of the original title. Baegun was a monk of the Korean Seon Buddhism school (the Korean equivalent of Zen Buddhism) who was active during the 14th century, or the late Goryeo period. He probably published the book in 1372. The gist of the book is in its lengthy title, which means the following: Written by Baegun, this is a record of the content of other books, a summary of teachings by the Buddha and revered Buddhist monks on *jikji simche* (teachings performed while pointing directly at the essence of the mind). Simply put, *Jikji* is Baegun's compilation of the essential content of books written by venerated monks throughout the history of Buddhism. Presumably, for future generations of monks, he compiled the most essential teachings from Seon Buddhist books too numerous to mention.

Jikji was printed with movable metal type in 1377 at Heungdeoksa Temple located on the outskirts of Cheongju, Chungcheongbuk-do Province, a fact that can be surmised from a passage within the book's postscript which states that *Jikji* was printed with movable metal type produced at this temple. However, nothing is known about what happened to the book after it was published. As is well known, *Jikji* remained hidden in obscurity until it was added to Collin de Plancy's personal collection. Its rediscovery happened in the 19th century, which means that the book was already more than 600 years old at the time. Yet, *Jikji* was in outstanding condition, and it is a wonder how this paper book had been preserved intact for such a long period. It is likely that *Jikji* was housed at a temple and that it was circulated among the monks or kept in a certain place. Since the book contains essential analects relevant to Seon practitioners, monks must have frequently read it. As such, it should have been worn out from use, but was not, which is hard to fathom. The book has most likely remained intact because the paper used was of exceptional quality. In fact, paper made in Goryeo was acknowledged as a premium product even in China. In any case, the book survived until Collin de Plancy discovered it during the late Joseon period, recognized its value, and took it to France. As we now know, the book is in good care at the National Library of France.

2. Events That Led to Park's Discovery of *Jikji*

Certainly, it was Collin de Plancy who played the most crucial role in Park's discovery of *Jikji*. As there is a chapter dedicated entirely to him, I will introduce him only briefly for the moment. It is said that despite being a French diplomat, he had no trouble comprehending Chinese texts because he majored in the Chinese language at the École des Langues Orientales Vivantes (School of Living Oriental Languages), a dedicated language institution established by the French Government. In this regard, it is indeed fortunate that the book was discovered by him as he must have immediately realized that it was not an ordinary book. At this point, we ask ourselves where *Jikji* had been kept until then (perhaps at a Buddhist temple?) as well as through which channel and broker it was delivered to Collin de Plancy. I am curious about what type of merchants dealt in old books and antiques at the time and how their national network was organized, but I will skip that particular discussion because this paper is not the proper venue for it.

I often give public lectures on *Jikji,* and every time I find that most Korean audiences are misinformed. When I ask them: "Did the French buy *Jikji* or steal it?" most would say, "it was stolen by the French." Then if I ask a second question: "Do you know where the book is today?" most of the audience would say, "It's at the Louvre Museum." Obviously, both answers are wrong. The Korean people are confused about what the French stole and what they legitimately took to France. The treasure they stole from Joseon is *Uigwe,* or the Royal Protocols of the Joseon Dynasty, and, as previously mentioned, it is housed at the National Library of France, not at a museum. As seen above, the Korean people are not particularly familiar with *Jikji* even though it is the world's oldest extant book printed with movable metal type and a part of their proud cultural heritage.

Once I inform my Korean audiences of the truth, I tell them that the Korean people must express gratitude toward the French because if the book had remained in Korea, it is highly likely that it would have been lost forever. The thing is, in the late 19th century, all aspects of Korean society, including politics and culture, were in a downward spiral, leaving the Korean people unable to focus their energy on maintaining their traditional culture. What's worse, during the subsequent decades, they had to live through a harsh Japanese colonial rule, followed by the terrible Korean War that lasted for three years (1950–1953), and then by breakneck economic development starting in the 1960s, all of which left no room for the preservation of traditional culture. Under these turbulent circumstances, there was a high chance that the book would have been lost. As previously mentioned, it is extremely rare for a book over 600 years old and in circulation among people (Buddhists) to be preserved to the present day. In my view, the book was rescued from its destiny of extinction thanks to its relocation to France in the early 20th century by Collin de Plancy. For this reason, we do not have the right to ask France to return the book. After all, they bought it through legitimate means and took it home with them.

Collin de Plancy returned to France with his collection of books and other artifacts. It is said that he donated his collection to the École des Langues Orientales Vivantes (School of Living Oriental Languages), his alma mater, but he probably did not donate *Jikji* and instead kept it for himself [4] because, presumably, he was well aware

---

4) According to Dr. Park, among Collin de Plancy's collection was *Hwaseong seongyeok uigwe* (Construction Records of Hwaseong Fortress). She informed Korean authorities

of the significance of the book.[5] Later, it is said that *Jikji* was auctioned off to Henri Vever (1854–1943) for the price of 180 francs. How much that price was worth is hard to ascertain. Although Park said it was of a considerable value, I have a feeling that 180 francs was still a relatively small amount of money. However, the book's new owner left a will requesting that his son donate the book to the National Library of France, suggesting that Vever also knew of the prime importance of this book, presumably from the information he obtained from what is written on the cover of *Jikji*. However, according to Park, the vibe at the time was that *Jikji* could not be believed to be the oldest movable metal type printed book just because of what it said on its cover. Probably, the book's relatively low auction price is a testament to the general atmosphere at the time. If the truth about *Jikji* had been officially recognized when Vever purchased the book, its price would have skyrocketed. However, no such recognition was forthcoming, suggesting that the book's preciousness had yet to be acknowledged at the time.

of this fact, but they did not show much interest, saying that Korea had another copy of the book. However, according to her, the copy housed at the National Library of France is of higher quality than its counterpart in Korea, as it features gilt and much clearer printing.

5) A theory has it that the book was on display at the Korean Pavilion of the 1900 Paris Exposition. However, since there is a counterargument, I have decided not to mention the theory. The counterargument appears in the following source.

Lee, S. (2009). *Ilh-ŏ-pŏ-lin chik-chi-lŭl ch'ach-a-sŏ* [In search of the lost Jikji] (pp. 215-216). Seoul, Korea: I-tam.

In the end, *Jikji* was acquired by the National Library of France, waiting to be rediscovered by Park. I have already discussed the reason why the book was ignored by the librarians at the time. Even though its front cover stated, in effect, that it was the oldest extant book printed with movable metal type, there had been no research to prove it, so *Jikji* had been left abandoned. In the following chapter, we will focus on Dr. Park Byeng-sen and her struggle.

III

Park Byeng-sen and *Jikji*

There are not very many resources that provide details on how Park, the so-called "godmother of *Jikji*," rediscovered the book and proved that it was printed with movable metal type. Here, her rigorous efforts to corroborate details are of particular importance. As previously mentioned, Collin de Plancy had already stated, in effect, that *Jikji* is the oldest movable metal type printed book, but the statement was without any verification. As such, validating that statement was the single most important remaining task, and was a task which Park took on. Yet, there is hardly any documentation by a third party on the process of her corroboration, and that is probably because the work took on a very personal dimension for her. For this reason, we cannot help but look to Park's own statements to examine how she conducted her verification process. If someone had closely followed her biographical trajectory and wrote a book about it, that would have been a reliable resource, but such a book does not exist. As such, we can only draw a rough sketch of the situation, based on her public lectures and press interviews.

As previously mentioned, it is very likely that the French librarians were unwilling to verify that *Jikji* is the oldest surviving book printed with movable metal type. Or more likely, they were simply not up to the task. It is unclear how proficient the librarians were in Chinese and how knowledgeable they were about old Chinese books, but it is likely they were not well versed in either area. In 1967, Park began to work as a librarian, albeit on a temporary basis, at the National Library of France because the library asked her to conduct research on Chinese-script books. It is said that the library staff noticed her, an Asian student who had been frequently visiting the library for research, and offered her a temporary job as a librarian working 15 hours a week. As such, it seems that the French librarians at the time were unfamiliar with Chinese books. If any of them had had adequate knowledge on the topic, it would not have been necessary for the library to hire an Asian female student even on a temporary basis.

As I surmise, even if some of the librarians were well versed in classical Chinese and ancient Chinese texts, they would not have been willing to prove that *Jikji* was the oldest book printed with movable metal type, for a variety of reasons. To begin with, as stated before, they would not have been able to imagine that an "uncivilized country" like Joseon was in fact the creator of such a cultural artifact of the highest caliber. Perhaps, they thought that such a feat was impossible and ignored the statement on the front cover of *Jikji*. They may have even thought that it was a Chinese book. Probably for such reasons, *Jikji* was discovered by Park in the archive of oriental manuscripts. It is highly likely that the French librarians thought *Jikji* was just an ordinary Chinese book, and therefore did not pay it much attention.

Another possible reason for their dismissal of the book is that it would have been an extremely challenging task to verify that *Jikji* was a book printed with movable metal type. Such verification would have required expert knowledge of the printing culture of China (and Japan) which belongs to the "Chinese character cultural sphere." However, it is doubtful that such an expert existed in the entire country of France, not to mention in the National Library of France. Considering that Collin De Plancy studied Chinese at the École des Langues Orientales Vivantes (School of Living Oriental Languages), there were presumably some French people well versed in the Chinese language; however, almost no French person would have been an expert in the printing culture associated with Chinese-script books. That is why *Jikji* had remained hidden in obscurity in the archive of oriental manuscripts, waiting for Park to disclose its momentous identity.

1. How Park Came to Encounter *Jikji*

Born in the 1920s, Park Byeng-sen (1926–2011) majored in history education at the College of Education, Seoul National University in the late 1940s.[6] She graduated in 1950 and went to Paris, France in 1955 as the first Korean female student to study in France through a sponsorship from the Korean Government. She graduated from Sorbonne University in 1959 and later in 1962 from the Catholic University of Leuven in Belgium. Then in 1971, she earned her PhD in history from Paris Diderot University (Paris 7) with a dissertation entitled "A Study on Korean Folklore through Historical Sites." Here, what matters is not where she studied and what she majored in but what course of events led to her rediscovery of *Jikji* while she was studying in France.

As the process of her discovery is fairly well-known and straightforward, it does not require much explanation. It is said that, before heading to France, her professor, Professor Lee Byeong-do, told her that the French Navy looted Korean books from the Oegyujanggak Royal Library during the French Disturbance of 1866. He then asked her to find the identities and whereabouts of the looted books. Professor Lee was one of the greatest Korean scholars at the

---

6) It is uncertain which department she graduated from because its name has since changed, but the important thing is that she majored in Korean history.

time. He was criticized for allegedly having been influenced by colonialist historiography, due to his involvement with the Society for the Compilation of Korean History under the Japanese Government General of Korea. Still, he is credited with expanding new horizons in Korean historiography. Here, a small question emerges: Professor Lee was a professor of the history department in the College of Liberal Arts and Sciences at Keijō Imperial University (present-day Seoul National University). In contrast, Park was a student of the College of Education of the same university. How, then, was Professor Lee able to approach a student of a different college and make such a suggestion?

The following is a possible scenario: It is highly likely that, as an undergraduate, Park took Professor Lee's class at the College of Liberal Arts and Sciences. In that case, they must have been acquainted, but it is still unclear how close their relationship actually was. Regardless, the announcement that Park would go to France in 1955 as a history student sponsored by the Korean Government must have been sensational news to people at the university. It was only two years after the Korean War, and Korea was one of the poorest countries in the world. As such, the news that a student would go to France, an advanced country, to continue her studies must have circulated not only throughout the College of Education but also throughout the College of Liberal Arts and Sciences. Thus, upon hearing the news, Professor Lee must have approached her and made the aforementioned academic suggestion.

At the time, historians in Korea knew that the French Navy looted royal books from the Oegyujanggak Royal Library. They knew the looted books were in France, but it seems that they did not know which books had in fact been looted. Since the historians knew what types of books had been housed at the library, they were able to make an educated guess, but did not know exactly which books were stolen by the French Navy, for France did not have any records related to the incident. It is probably for this reason that Professor Lee asked Park to conduct relevant research in France. In those days, going abroad was a privilege rarely extended even to professors, not to mention ordinary people. Besides, searching for the looted books would have taken a long period of time, incurring huge expenses. As such, researchers in charge of the mission would not have been able to stay long enough in France. It is probably for these reasons that Professor Lee asked a history student heading to France to conduct further studies to search for the looted books.

It seems that, at the time, Park read from Maurice Courant's *Korean Bibliography* that the books acquired during the French Disturbance of 1866 were all donated to the National Library of France and later became determined to find those books. Then in 1967, as previously mentioned, the library offered her a job as a librarian, so she probably accepted the job offer, thinking that it would give her an opportunity to search for those books. Keeping this in mind, she immediately began her research and happened to come across *Jikji* on the very first year of her employment, without being able to locate the books looted from the Oegyujanggak Royal Library. It is said that *Jikji* had been sitting in the archive of Chinese manuscripts, completely abandoned and covered with dust. It appears that she found *Jikji* while searching for the looted books in that archive.

At long last, *Jikji* fell into Park's hands. What was it like when she first discovered the book? She must have known about the existence of the book through *Korean Bibliography*, but without knowing its whereabouts. As such, it is hard to imagine how delighted she was when she encountered *Jikji* in the library. Not even in her wildest dreams would she have imagined that the book was in this library. We can imagine how she felt when she discovered the book and read on its postscript the passage "*cheongjumogoe heungdeoksa jujainsi*" (printed with cast metal type in Heungdeoksa Temple outside the Cheongju region), and then realized that the *cheongju* mentioned therein is today's Cheongju City in Chungcheongbuk-do Province, the Republic of Korea. At that moment, she immediately recognized the possibility that the book was the world's oldest movable metal type printed book, but she also knew that she could not announce her discovery as fact based merely on what Collin de Plancy or Courant claimed, for such a claim had to be substantiated by an elaborate verification process. To make matters worse, there had been no historical record proving the existence of Heungdeoksa Temple on the outskirts of Cheongju, which must have made it even more difficult to confidently argue that *Jikji* was published at the temple.[7]

2. Verification Process of the Metal Type Printing of *Jikji*

According to Park, at first, she did not realize that the book was the sole copy. She thought that, since *Jikji* was printed with movable metal type, there would have been other copies. But even so, proving that it was printed with movable metal type would verify that it is the oldest extant book of its kind, produced 78 years earlier than Gutenberg's Bible. It is said that Collin de Plancy, Courant, and Vever all used to say that "If" this book is genuine, it would be the world's oldest movable metal type printed book, always emphasizing the word "if." Even though the book's postscript states that it was printed with movable metal type, people would not have believed the statement. As previously mentioned, Europeans, in particular, would not have

---

7) Surprisingly, the site for Heungdeoksa Temple was discovered by chance in 1985 at a housing development site in today's Cheongju City, thereby establishing the printing of *Jikji* at the temple as a firm fact.

wanted to believe that. Perhaps, for this reason, when Park told her colleagues at work that *Jikji* was the oldest extant book printed with movable metal type, they considered it nonsense and completely disagreed with her.

Deeply disturbed by such reactions, she sent letters to acquaintances in Korea, asking for help. However, when she asked if there were any research findings or newspaper articles in Korea regarding movable metal type, they did not show much interest. In these circumstances, it was obvious that no one had previously conducted research on this topic, and such realization let her down completely. Park recalled that she felt discouraged partly because metal printing was not her field of research and because she was afraid of learning about it, not to mention being discouraged by the lack of existing research. Wasn't it only natural for her to feel that way? It would be a momentous historic event that would rewrite a page in the history of the world to establish that *Jikji* was printed with movable metal type, 78 years before the printing of the Gutenberg Bible. However, under such adverse circumstances, she was understandably disheartened.

At the time, she must have felt the weight of the world upon her shoulders, a sense of being all alone at the center stage of history. In similar circumstances, ordinary people would have succumbed to such emotional pressure and avoided becoming involved in the situation. Verifying that *Jikji* is printed with movable metal type must have been a real challenge in and of itself, but when she considered the repercussions of such verification, it must have been even harder for her to muster up the courage required. If her corroboration succeeded, Europe (more specifically Germany) would lose the tile of being the inventor of metal type, so Europeans would never accept such fact without putting up a fight.

However, fortunately for us, Park took up the challenge of validating the fact that *Jikji* was printed with movable metal type. There are no documents detailing how she came to that resolution; instead, we can only partially surmise the circumstances from what she recalled during her public lecture.[8] Since there were no relevant resources available in Korea, she collected resources from China and Japan. Fortunately, as a Korean history major, she had a good command of Chinese and Japanese. Still, reading a classical Chinese text is usually a time-consuming activity. It is unclear which resources she read or how she did it, but Park says that it took a "humongous" amount of time. At the time, she was working on her PhD while also working at the library, leaving her with insufficient time to conduct research on ancient printing type.

---

8) The lecture was held at the Korea National University of Cultural Heritage, under the title "The Significance and Meaning of *Jikji*" on October 20, 2010 as part of the university's Baekgang Special Lecture Series.

Regarding the circumstances at the time, Park said at a press interview[9] that, to secure a maximum amount of time for her research, she reduced the time she spent eating and sleeping, consuming only bread and coffee. At the same time, she reduced her level of physical activity to sustain herself with such a small amount of food. According to Park, she concentrated on her research so much (and therefore became absent-minded) that she would often go to a market, buy just one of the many items she had planned to buy and return home, thinking that she had bought everything she needed. As suggested in the above anecdote, she embarked on a rigorous study of metal printing and relevant theories through books. However, she felt that this alone was not sufficient.

After pondering this problem, she visited foundries around her home and observed the process of casting metal. However, she soon realized that mere observation was not enough, so she decided to make metal type herself. To this end, she performed several tasks. Since she has discussed them on diverse media outlets, the exact order of these tasks is unclear. However, what matters is not the order, but the concerted efforts she had to make to verify that *Jikji* was printed with movable metal type. She obtained from printing houses and newspaper companies in Paris molds used to make metal type

9) Lee, E. (2011, December 23). *'Chik-chi-ŭi tae-mo' ko pak-pyŏng-sŏn pak-sa-ŭi il-saeng* [Life of the late Dr. Park Byeng-Sen, godmother of Jikji] *Women News*.

and tried making her own lead type. She probably wanted to see how a text on a piece of paper looks when printed with movable metal type. It is said that, during such experiments, she ended up starting a fire at her residence three times, probably while she was melting lead and pouring it into the mold. Sometimes, she used an eraser or potato to make simple type. It is said that she also made type using soil. They needed to be burned in a ceramic oven, which, of course, she did not have, so she burned them in a regular oven in her kitchen and ended up breaking the oven three times. One day, she also ended up breaking a window, thereby inviting complaints from her landlord. Here, I wonder how she broke the oven and window. Did the oven explode? If so, she must have had to compensate the landlord for the damage. However, she did not mention any subsequent details, so there is no way to know for sure. Anyway, through a series of experiments, she finally succeeded in understanding the difference between type and woodblock as well as the differences among wooden-type, clay-type (which is made by burning soil), and metal-type printings.[10]

As we have just seen, she conducted research and experiments by taking time out of her busy schedule. She would often stay up all night, and go to work red-eyed. Then her colleagues would ask if she

10) Park, B (2002). Author's preface. In *Han-kuk-ŭi in-swae* [Korean printing]. Cheongju, Korea: Cheongju Early Printing Museum Press.

had cried the previous night. It is through such painstaking endeavor that she was able to disclose *Jikji's* secrets. It is unclear how long her research and experiments continued, but they presumably lasted until the book was released to the public during a book exhibition held in celebration of the International Book Year of 1972, meaning that she conducted research for a period of up to five years. Tracing the trajectory of her research and experiments, I have been astonished at how tenacious human resolve can be. A layperson who knew nothing about movable type became an expert in metal type printing through research and personal experiments, thereby achieving a singular remarkable feat. Besides, her work was not aimed at publishing a research outcome for a small academic association; it was about changing the perspective of people around the world on the subject. We cannot even imagine the emotional burden she had to carry.

After such arduous research, Park became confident that *Jikji* was printed with movable metal type, and now waited for a chance to proclaim the fact to the world. Then, as previously mentioned, a book exhibition was held at the National Library of France in 1972, under the auspices of UNESCO. She decided to utilize this event for her cause, but the library felt that it was insolent for her to push the idea. The organization also took great pains to decide whether or not to display the book because if experts accepted *Jikji* as a book printed with movable metal type, this would be a great honor to the library, but if Park's verification proved to be false, the library would be open to criticism. In response to such concern, Park is said to have insisted that she would take all the blame, asking the library to direct the blame toward her if something went wrong. She was able to insist on this precondition because her thorough research and experiments over the years had given her the requisite confidence.

Eventually, the exhibition was opened to the public. At first, people just passed by the book, but experts soon realized that it was not an ordinary book and began to talk amongst themselves. For about a month afterward, they would come to her and request a detailed explanation. Without being overwhelmed by such requests, she presented the experts with all of her research findings. And they began to accept her ideas. She says that, during that month, she was unable to do anything else except spend time answering their questions. The exhibition was soon followed by an academic conference on oriental studies. She attended the conference and made a presentation on *Jikji*, arguing that it was a book printed in Korea with movable metal type, 78 years before the printing of the Gutenberg Bible. However, her argument was met with heavy criticism from other attendees, which was exactly as expected. For starters, since many Western scholars tend to be meticulous and persistent, their questions must have been as sharp as knives. On top of that, since the issue was a matter of pride for Europeans, they must have been unwilling to readily acknowledge that *Jikji* is the world's oldest extant book printed with movable metal type. For this reason, they must have aggressively asked pointed questions. According to Park, it was not only scholars but also printing professionals, publishers, and journalists who posed critical questions to her. Perhaps, her discovery was so momentous that their collective pride was on the verge of falling apart. She is said to have been under a lot of stress amidst such circumstances. However, she presented these scholars, printing experts, and journalists with countless pieces of evidence in an impressively confident manner, garnering acceptance of her claims in the end. Eventually, Park's rediscovery was recognized by the global academic community, which resulted in the inscription *Jikji* on UNESCO's Memory of the World Register in 2001.[11]

3. Evidence that *Jikji* Was Printed with Movable Metal Type

So far, we have examined how *Jikji* came to be recognized as the world's oldest extant book printed with movable metal type. Now, we

---

11) There is another reminiscence of Dr. Park. When President Chun Doo-hwan, the incumbent president of Korea at the time, visited France, President Mitterrand of France showed him a photographic edition of *Jikji,* while saying that he respects the president of a country with such splendid cultural heritage. President Chun is said to have been very pleased at this. Upon returning to Korea, he ordered the construction of an exhibition hall in Cheongju, which later became Cheongju Early Printing Museum.

need only to delve into how Park was able to prove this fact. Currently, there is no single resource providing a compilation of information on this matter. As such, I have collected fragmented information from books and Park's interviews to present a comprehensive picture of the process in this chapter.

The following content is based on Park's book *Korean Printing.*[12] Each page of *Jikji* consists of 11 vertical lines, with each line containing 18–20 characters. The spacing of the 18-character lines and the spacing of the 20-character lines are different, which makes the characters look misaligned horizontally, unlike characters printed with woodblock. In the case of woodblock printing, a piece of paper with writing on it is attached to a woodblock, and then the spaces around the characters are carved out to create a relief. As a result, characters printed with woodblock are well aligned both vertically and horizontally. However, in the case of movable metal type printing, since each line has a different number of characters in it, the size, thickness, and location of characters may not be consistent. The same kind of misalignment has been found in annotations which appear six times throughout the book. The annotations each feature two lines with small-sized characters. These characters also appear misaligned

---

12) Park, B (2002). *Han-kuk-ŭi in-swae* [Korean printing] (pp. 87–88). Cheongju, Korea: Cheongju Early Printing Museum Press.

just as in regular texts. Such horizontal misalignment suggests that printing and metal casting technologies at the time were yet to be perfected. Besides, since Heungdeoksa Temple was just an ordinary temple, it is likely that movable metal type made there were of subpar quality.

Such lack of sophistication is also apparent in other aspects. For instance, sometimes the bottom portion of a character overlaps with the top portion of the following character. Moreover, since a different amount of Chinese ink was rubbed onto each movable metal type, each printed character displays a different degree of thickness and darkness. There are also some ink stains on the book. According to Park, these stains have been left on the pages because the printers did not have the necessary technology to remove them. I feel unfortunate that I have not had the chance to actually observe this phenomenon myself directly. As for movable metal types, there is evidence that some metal types were modified with scissors, which probably occurred because the printers had a shortage of movable metal types and therefore had to recycle the existing types to make new ones. Finally, there are specks on the book caused by metal debris that was near the types. Park says that these specks are strong evidence that *Jikji* was printed with movable metal type. The thing is, the printers were supposed to remove metal debris before printing, but somehow they failed to do so, leaving specks on the book.

Park also talks about the style of calligraphy. *Jikji* features the Songxue style created by Calligrapher Zhao Mengfu of the Yuan Dynasty, which was popular in Korea during the late Goryeo period. This fact matches the time period of the printing of *Jikji* mentioned in the book itself. Another piece of evidence Park paid attention to was the use of an ancient Korean script known as *idu*. The idu script was placed next to Chinese characters to facilitate comprehension. Idu changed with time, and, according to Park, the type of idu used in *Jikji* has the characteristics of the variation used during the Goryeo period.[13] It was through these pieces of strong evidence that she was able to make her claim that *Jikji* was printed with movable metal type during the late Goryeo period.

In one of her lectures, Park presented yet more interesting evidence regarding *Jikji*. She took photographs of the same character appearing on different pages and enlarged them for comparison. The result: they looked exactly the same. If these same characters had been printed with woodblock, each of them would have been slightly different, but they are exactly the same in appearance, suggesting that they were printed with movable metal type. The thing is, since a woodblock is

---

13) For this, I have consulted the following academic paper.
   Nam, P. (1999). Chik-chi-sim-ch'e-yo-chŏl-ŭi ku-kyŏl [The use of oral instructions in Jikji] In *Kuk-ŏ-sa-lŭl wi-han ku-kyŏl yŏn-ku* [A study on gugyeol (oral instructions) for the history of the Korean language] (pp. 433–464). Seoul, Korea: T'ae-hak-sa.

made by hand, the same characters appearing in different places may look slightly different. However, there are no such discrepancies in *Jikji*. It was previously mentioned that Park carried out experiments on printing with types made of potato, radish, eraser and other materials, to see how each type produces different prints. According to her, characters printed with these materials looked similar to one another, when viewed in their original sizes; however, they looked slightly different from one another, when enlarged 50 times. It was through such experiments that Park was able to deduce the visual characteristics of movable metal type printing. She also mentioned facts about ancient papers. According to her, paper used during the Silla, Goryeo and early Joseon period in Korea were all different. The paper used for *Jikji* was clearly not paper made in Joseon; however, it was identical to the type of paper used in an ancient Japanese book known to have been produced with paper made in Goryeo.

Don't all these pieces of evidence constitute proof beyond a reasonable doubt that *Jikji* was, as stated in its postscript, printed with movable metal type at Heungdeoksa Temple located in the outskirts of Cheongju in 1377? Perhaps that is why Park was able to act with such confidence in front of all those experts. Otherwise, it would have been impossible to persuade each and every one of those Western experts. Confronted by the hard evidence Park presented, those experts were left with no choice but to accept her argument.

IV

Closing Remarks

So far, we have discussed a fair number of stories related to Dr. Park Byeng-sen and *Jikji,* so there is not much else to add to this discussion. However, it would be regrettable if I wrapped up this paper without mentioning her other achievements. Rediscovering *Jikji* and verifying that it was the oldest movable metal type printed book was only one of her broad list of achievements. As well-known, her original objective was to rediscover books looted from the Oegyujanggak Royal Library of Joseon. In fact, her efforts paid off when she finally discovered *Uigwe,* or the Royal Protocols of the Joseon Dynasty in 1975 at an archive of the National Library of France. Through her passionate efforts, *Uigwe* was returned to Korea in the form of a permanent loan, a somewhat unfortunate solution. In fact, the return process was replete with dramatic stories. Here is one well-known anecdote: When she discovered *Uigwe* and told her colleagues in the library about it, they treated her like a traitor, giving her the cold shoulder and eventually forcing her to quit her job. Notably, even Korean government authorities exhibited unfriendliness toward her. It is said that they criticized her severely, asking her to leave things as they were instead of creating an elephant in the room.

I did not cover such stories in detail here for obvious reasons, for this paper focuses solely on her accounts associated with *Jikji*. Unfortunately, talking about her stories related to *Uigwe* and her lifelong achievement needs to be deferred. The breadth of her research was so wide that, perhaps, her other stories must be included in a book-length biography dedicated to her achievements. Given that, the discovery of *Jikji* and related research are her foremost achievement. As a matter of fact, when it comes to *Uigwe,* since Korea also possessed another copy, the rarity value of this collection of books is not particularly high. It is true that the *Uigwe* returned from France to Korea is more valuable than its Korean counterpart because the former contains parts dedicated to special viewing by the king. Still, in terms of the cultural history of humanity, *Jikji* is of greater value than *Uigwe* for reasons we have already discussed. Moving forward, Dr. Park Byeng-sen will be remembered as a great woman who rediscovered *Jikji* and proved that it was the world's oldest surviving book printed with movable metal type.

Generalization   Oh Youngtack
Planning   Lee Jun-koo
Text   Choi Junsik / Lee Hye-Eun
Edition   Jang won-yeon
Translation   Kim Hyo-jeong, Kim Yong-hee

Date of publication   20th December 2019
Publisher   Cheongju city / Cheongju Early Printing Museum

Cheongju Early Printing Museum
Address 713, Jikjidaero, Heungdeok-gu, Cheongju city,
Chungbuk Province, South Korea
Tel 043-201-4298 / Fax 043-201-4299
http://jikjiworld.cheongju.go.kr
Printer   Ilgwang Co., Ltd
12, 204Bungil, Sangdangro, Sangdang-gu, Cheongju city,
Chungbuk Province, South Korea
Tel 043-221-2948

Registration number of publication   73-5710016-000011-14
ISBN   978-89-6771-154-2 94740

94060

9 788967 711542
ISBN 978-89-6771-154-2
ISBN 978-89-6771-098-9 (세트)

緣化

門人　釋璨
　　　遠湛

施主

比丘尼　妙德

名為智膝入覽不思議

承古裡師常勸諸人莫學佛法但自然心夬利根

人盡時經脫鈍根人或三五年遂不過十年若大

悟去老僧替你入拔舌

白雲和尚抄錄佛祖直指心體要節卷下

寺鑄字印施

宣光七年丁巳七月　日　清州牧外興德